Twayne's English Authors Series

Sylvia E. Bowman, *Editor*

INDIANA UNIVERSITY

Harold Pinter

 51

Harold Pinter

By Arnold P. Hinchliffe
University of Manchester (England)

Twayne Publishers, Inc.   ::   New York

To
MY MOTHER

Preface

In the preface to *Experimental Drama*, a symposium published in 1963, W. A. Armstrong explained the vitality of contemporary British drama as the meeting between imagination and complacency: "Beckett's enigmatic Godot has sent a religious tremor through a predominantly secular age; Pinter's haunted heroes have been a salutary reminder of what we still have to face when the Welfare State has done its best (or worst) for us; the tirades of Osborne's Jimmy Porter and the snide patter of his Archie Rice have emboldened the young and goaded their elders: Behan's Quare Fellow looms insistently over the issue of capital punishment: Bolt's Sir Thomas More, O'Casey's Father Ned, and Wesker's Beatie Bryant have likewise spoken to the conscience through the medium of the play."

Since 1956, it has been habitual to think of the British theater as once more vital and promising; whether or not the habit stemmed from an enthusiasm assumed by English critics as a relief from boredom and to assuage national pride (as George E. Wellwarth suggests in *The Theater of Protest and Paradox*), it is a habit that had so grown upon readers and critics alike that Bamber Gascoigne's 1964 New Year's article in *The Observer*, "Keeping Up with the Crisis," came as something of a shock. In it he reminded us that 1963 had produced not one new striking play: "The present score of dramatists seems to read: Osborne lost to films, Delaney silent, Behan indisposed, no full-length work from Pinter for over three years. Was it all a flash in a pan, the great new British drama?"[1]

In fact, Kenneth Tynan in *Tynan on Theater* (reprinted, 1963) had anticipated this view, and John Russell Taylor echoed it in *Plays and Players* (August, 1964) in an article entitled, "What's Happened to the New Dramatists?" A hiatus of this kind is certainly disturbing, but then, as Gascoigne pointed out, 1594 was also a bad year: Thomas Kyd was dead without living up to his promise; Christopher Marlowe had been killed in somewhat unsavory circumstances; and Robert Greene was dead of over-indulgence. Only William Shakespeare was left, a dramatist who had shown signs of promise but had then gone commercial by writing a huge star part for Richard Burbage in *Richard III*. It was encouraging to remember in the quatercentenary year of 1964 that 1594 had also seemed a black year for the British theater.

Of all the British dramatists who have emerged to produce this sense of a new, vital British theater, Harold Pinter seems to me the most interesting and significant. I hope the following pages will illustrate why I believe this to be so and will justify writing about a dramatist who is, I hope, only at the beginning of his career and who will continue to produce plays for the stage. It seems to me that the business of criticism is to dive in as soon as possible, especially when simple plays prove so apparently puzzling. Wellwarth has suggested that the very complexity of contemporary drama obliges critics to work at it while it is still alive—indeed, before it even comes to life—rather than wait to chart it as a movement in history. Such an obligation may exist, but my feeling is that the complexity as such is after the event, that an audience can enjoy Pinter immensely (if its reaction during performance is anything to go by) and only on leaving the charmed atmosphere of the auditorium does it qualify that enjoyment with the awful question: "But what did it mean?" As if, in fact, one or two hours of enjoyment do not themselves constitute a kind of meaning.

Terence Rattigan's reported exchange with Pinter is an example of this secondary response: "When I saw *The Caretaker* I told Pinter that I knew what it meant. 'It's about the God of the Old Testament, the God of the New, and Humanity, isn't it?' Pinter said blankly, 'No, Terry, it's about a caretaker and two brothers.'" Similarly, when rehearsing the recent production of *The Lover*, Pinter is reported to have said: "We're not quite sure of the author's intention here." Neither of these cases rings untrue, nor, I am sure, are they examples of authorial perversity, either conscious or unconscious. In a radio interview with Laurence Kitchin, Pinter described his own running commentary on the plays as a complete waste of time. He has to come to his own plays objectively like anyone else: "I don't want to sound a mystificator, if there's a word, but I really do not know what . . . is in the script from A to Z by any means. I think it would be an impertinence of me to say that I did . . . as a director my function is really to look at the text quite independently and objectively really and truly and the only thing is I do of course . . . happen to have something of the certain inner word. I mean someone. I know a little more. I've got something out of the horse's mouth. I've got a hot tip you know. . . ."

Pinter has always insisted that his plays are simple and straightforward, and so they are until confronted with the question of specific meaning, by which people generally mean allegory. This book is partly the history of that particular question, partly a history of very recent British drama as Pinter has contributed to it, and partly a history of his personal development as a dramatist. It is also in many ways a history of a developing tolerance of his method. One of the remarkable things about his short career is the fact that within the space of five years or so, a dramatist who had been almost universally dismissed by drama critics is now accepted as one of the leading dramatists of the day. Laurence Kitchin sees him as the most accomplished dramatist of the 1960's so far, a view supported by John Russell Taylor. For Joseph Chiari, Pinter is more versatile and more gifted and is a better craftsman than any of his contemporaries and, with the possible exception of John Arden, is likely to outdistance all of them.

In 1964, John Russell Brown took another look at Shakespeare in the light of Pinter's plays. But not all critics are converted, of course. Allardyce Nicoll, in his revised *British Drama* (1962), included the Theater of the Absurd for the first time; he devoted six lines to N. F. Simpson, merely mentioned Pinter, and described *Waiting for Godot* as "the much-discussed and somewhat repetitively boring" play. Each critic is subject to personal taste, naturally; but when Nicoll described R. C. Sherrif's play *The Long Sunset* (1955) as thoughtful, it is clear that taste can restrict judgment too excessively.[2]

In short, Pinter has already produced enough that is interesting, significant, and well done to deserve some sort of critical attention, albeit of an elementary kind. This little history intends to be nothing more than an elementary introduction.

Harold Pinter is quintessentially the English (I am tempted to say "London") representative of Absurd Theater. He has incorporated the genre so successfully that it is almost parochial in flavor and looks decidedly home-grown. This ability to fuse European Absurdity with the English way of life, the foreign with the native, the timeless and universal with the immediate and local, gives Pinter's plays a lasting quality. He will remain one of Britain's most important twentieth-century dramatists— in my opinion, the most important.

ARNOLD P. HINCHLIFFE

Manchester, 1966

Acknowledgments

I am deeply indebted to Harold Pinter, not merely for permission to use unpublished and broadcast material, but also for the interest he has shown in the work as it proceeded. I should also like to thank Joseph Losey and Warner Pathé (for help in connection with *The Servant*); Iain Hamilton (for sending me the first publication of "A Slight Ache"); Alan Hancox (for assistance in tracking down Pinter's poetry); Peter Wait and Methuen's for continued assistance with the published texts of Pinter; the Staff of the British Museum Reading Room (for research into the first publication of "The Examination"); and John Kershaw of A.T.V. Ltd., for the script of the *Tempo* program in October, 1965.

I must also thank Zdzislaw Mikulski for his translation of the article by Grzegorz Sinko, and Professor Sinko for permission to use the article, and my colleague F. N. Lees for permission to quote from his paper on Samuel Beckett.

I wish to acknowledge the part played by the work of Martin Esslin and John Russell Taylor, which far exceeds what is recorded in the footnotes, and that, in the opening chapter, I have been much influenced by Raymond Williams' essay on contemporary drama.

I also wish to thank David Hirst and Andrew P. Debicki, who have found texts and criticisms for me, and finally, John Davidson, who typed, corrected, retyped, and recorrected the text.

The following permissions to quote from and refer to published works are acknowledged:

From *Stratford-on-Avon Studies*, No. 4, edited by J. R. Brown and B. Harris, for chapters by Clifford Leech and R. D. Smith. Copyright © Edward Arnold (Publishers), Ltd.

From *Experimental Drama*, edited by W. A. Armstrong, for essays by W. A. Armstrong, Geoffrey Bullough and Martin Esslin. Copyright © 1963 by G. Bell and Sons, Ltd.

From *The Dark Comedy*, by J. L. Styan. Copyright © 1962 by Cambridge University Press.

From "Mr. Pinter's Shakespeare," by John Russell Brown, by permission of the editor, *Critical Quarterly*, V. 3.

From *The Theater of the Absurd*, by Martin Esslin. Copyright © by Martin Esslin. Reprinted by permission of Doubleday & Company, Inc.

From *The Birthday Party*, review by Irving Wardle in *Encore* (July-August, 1958), by permission of the editors.

From *The Kitchen Sink*, by G. Wilson Knight in *Encounter* (December, 1963), by permission of the editor.

From *Mid-Century Drama*, by Laurence Kitchin. Copyright © by Faber and Faber, Ltd.

From "Joseph Losey and The Servant," by Jacques Brunius in *Film*, 38, by permission of the editor.

From "The Theater of the Absurd—How Absurd?" by David Tutaev in *Gambit*, by permission of the editor.

From *Twentieth Century Drama*, by Bamber Gascoigne. Copyright © by The Hutchinson Publishing Company.

From the plays of Harold Pinter. Copyright © Harold Pinter. Reprinted by permission of Grove Press, Inc., and Methuen & Co., Ltd.

From *Anger and After*, by John Russell Taylor. Copyright © by John Russell Taylor, reprinted by permission of Methuen & Co., Ltd.

From *Modern Drama*, for the articles by J. T. Boulton, "Harold Pinter: The Caretaker and Other Plays" (September, 1963), and J. Hoefer, "Pinter and Whiting: Two Attitudes Towards the Alienated Artist" (February, 1962), by permission of the editor.

From *New Theater Magazine*, for the article by Harold Pinter, "Harold Pinter Replies" (January, 1961), and the John Arden review of *The Caretaker* (July, 1960), by permission of the editor.

From *The Theater of Protest and Paradox*, by G. E. Wellwarth. Copyright © by New York University Press.

From *New English Dramatists*, No. 3, by J. W. Lambert, by permission of Penguin Books, Ltd.

From *Nausea*, by Jean-Paul Sartre, translated by Lloyd Alexander, by permission of the publishers, New Directions.

From *Sexual Deviations*, by Anthony Storr, by permission of Penguin Books, Ltd.

Acknowledgments

From an interview on filming *The Caretaker* in *Transatlantic Review*, No. 13, by permission of the editor.

From *Tulane Drama Review*, for articles by Ruby Cohn, "The World of Harold Pinter" (March, 1962), and Bernard Dukore, "The Theater of Harold Pinter" (March, 1962), by permission of the editor.

From *Twentieth Century*, for "Writing for Myself," by permission of Harold Pinter and the editor.

From *Existentialism from Dostoevsky to Sartre*, by Walter Kaufmann. Copyright © by The World Publishing Company.

From *Sartre*, by Iris Murdoch. By permission of Yale University Press.

Contents

Preface

Acknowledgments

Chronology   17

1. The New Theater   21

2. Comedies of Menace   38

3. *The Caretaker*   87

4. Plays for Television   108

5. Interim Report   125

6. *The Homecoming*   146

7. Conclusion   163

Notes and References   166

Selected Bibliography   176

Index   185

Chronology

1930 Harold Pinter born in Hackney, London; only child of Jewish parents. Educated at Hackney Downs Grammar School. Entered Royal Academy of Dramatic Art, but finally faked nervous breakdown and left. Two trials as conscientious objector.

1949– Repertory actor under the name of David Baron; spent
1957 eighteen months with McMaster's company in Ireland.

1956 Married Vivien Merchant.

1957 *The Room, The Birthday Party,* and *The Dumb Waiter* written.

1957– Bristol University productions of *The Room.* Cambridge
1958 Arts Theatre production of *The Birthday Party,* which later ran for less than a week at the Lyric Theatre, Hammersmith.

1959 *A Slight Ache,* British Broadcasting Corporation, "Third Program," July 29th. "The Examination," published in *Prospect* (Summer, 1959). *Pieces of Eight,* Apollo Theatre, London, September 3rd, contained: "Getting Acquainted," "Request Stop," "Special Offer," and "Last to Go." *One to Another,* Lyric Opera House, Hammersmith, transferred to the Apollo Theatre, contained: "The Black and White" and "Trouble in the Works."

1960 *The Room* and *The Dumb Waiter* (first performed at Frankfurt Municipal Theatre) produced at Hampstead Theatre Club, January 21st, and later in March at the Royal Court Theatre. *A Night Out,* British Broadcasting Corporation, "Third Program," March 1st, and Independent Television Authority, April 24th. *The Caretaker,* Arts Theatre, London, April 27th, and the Duchess Theatre on May 30th. *Night School,* Independent Television Authority, July 21st. *The Dwarfs,* British Broadcasting Corporation, "Third Program," December 2nd.

1961 *A Slight Ache,* Arts Theatre, January 18th. *The Collection,* Independent Television Authority, May 11th.

1962   *The Collection*, Aldwych Theater, June 18th.

1963   *The Caretaker*, filmed in Hackney. *The Lover*, Independent Television Authority, March 28th. *The Lover* and *The Dwarfs*, Arts Theatre, London, September 16th. "The Examination," republished with *The Lover* and *The Collection*. "Dialogue for Three," *Stand*, Vol. VI, No. 3 (n.d.). Script for the film *The Servant* directed by Joseph Losey. Script for *The Pumpkin Eater* directed by Jack Clayton. Script for film not yet produced, *The Compartment*. Short story "Tea Party" broadcast British Broadcasting Corporation in 1964.

1964   New sketches broadcast, British Broadcasting Corporation, "Third Program."

1965   *Tea Party*, March 25th, British Broadcasting Corporation Television (and throughout Europe). *The Homecoming*, Cardiff, March 26th, presented by the Royal Shakespeare Company.

1966   Awarded C.B.E. Birthday Honours List. Script for *The Quiller Memorandum*, directed by Michael Anderson; script for *Accident*, directed by Joseph Losey.

1967   *The Basement* (originally film-script entitled *The Compartment*) February 20th. British Broadcasting Corporation Television Channel 2. Received Antoinette Perry Award for *The Homecoming*, the best Broadway Drama of 1966.

Harold Pinter

CHAPTER 1

The New Theater

"At any streetcorner the feeling of absurdity can strike any man in the face."—Camus

THE PARTICULAR KIND of theater with which we are concerned is that in which two or three characters meet for the purpose of talking to themselves. This situation is seen in the plays of Samuel Beckett, Harold Pinter, Edward Albee—and even in the late play by Eugene O'Neill called *Hughie.*[1] It is a trend in contemporary theater, and Pinter is its English representative; and it is the trend that, it seems to me, has most to say and do in the so-called revival of the British theater. There have been, of course, so many revivals in that perennial institution that it is difficult to believe that the theater had time to fade and die between them. The recent important revivals can be summed up, with varying adequacy, under the three headings of "Poetic," "Angry," and "Absurd"; and all three have also been concerned with the physical aspects of the theater—from the kind of stage to be used to such minor details as the abolition of footlights and curtains.

Some of this interest is a mitigated response to Brecht's theories of staging and alienation and is not remarkably important. As J. L. Styan has pertinently remarked in connection with Brecht: "In spite of everything, the flexibility of a willing spectator's imagination in conditions of theater resists the naked exposure of actuality. The dream world of illusory theater develops and proceeds as before, and pathetic overtones inevitably arise wherever there is a hint of sentiment."[2] Experiments to thwart the willing suspension of disbelief are either resented or are too successful with the average audience; and that audience is very important, for more than any other form of fiction, drama is a public activity in which the creation only comes to life under certain conditions, the most pressing of which is an audience willing to pay for it.

According to Raymond Williams in an essay about the contemporary theater, the economic pressure of an audience leads to two kinds of theater, majority and minority.[3] The minority (or free) theater rarely lasts for more than a few seasons but is important because it dares to stage something new in the way of drama. The majority theater is prosperous because it gives its audience precisely what it thinks it wants to see: spectacle, melodrama, or farce, and, in the other direction, sentimental comedy or domestic intrigue. Williams admits that the snobbery of a majority theater audience can ensure a favorable reception to any experimental play once it has the reputation of being "chic," but it is usually the little theater that establishes that reputation. An alternative, of course, would be for an established theatrical figure to throw the weight of his reputation behind a new play, but this is a double-edged gamble at the best of times. What is exciting recently is that a number of dramatists seem to have fooled or shocked the majority theater into accepting their plays as if they had been written according to conventional specifications. Williams might well have cited the respectable precedent of Shakespeare.

The first direct revolt against the requirements of the paying audience of the majority theater was verse drama, which, until about the 1950's, seemed the most hopeful trend away from the stale and uncreative. This drama seemed to be going somewhere, but it never got there. This failure may very well be due to the fact that these plays were the products of writers rather than dramatists. These writers, usually poets, wanted to widen the audience for their work by moving into the theater, feeling that only by using the widest range of human language—poetry— could they hope to capture the fullest contrasts and more intense moments of experience from which the moral lesson of drama emerges.

In its earliest stages, verse drama was the result of a gradual interest on the part of poets seeking new kinds of dramatic action. It can be traced from the work of William Butler Yeats and Ezra Pound with the Japanese Noh plays or in T. S. Eliot's unfinished dramatic poem, *Sweeney Agonistes*. But there were few, if any, theaters willing to experiment. Eliot's attempts were

[22]

more successful, dating from his first drama, *Murder in the Cathedral* (1935). In this play, however, Eliot was using Canterbury Cathedral as a theater; there he could rely not only on an audience, but on one habituated to fancy dress and to ritualistic language. When he turned to the commercial theater and to contemporary non–fancy-dress action, he ran into difficulties. From *The Family Reunion* (1939) to *The Elder Statesman* (1958), we can trace a steady movement away from attempting non-realistic action and from using verse-speech for its originally stated purpose.

In short, it proved difficult, if not impossible, to combine in this day and age natural action with dramatic blank verse. Although the audience or congregation at Canterbury found verse and action *natural* in that context, the commercial theater audience naturally required in drama the paraphernalia of life—telephones, umbrellas, and cocktails. It is perhaps asking too much of an author or actor to produce verse of any intensity while answering the telephone, finding a lost umbrella, or mixing a cocktail; and the spectator comes to feel that these things are there not for the purpose of the drama but simply to persuade the audience that, despite all evidence to the contrary, it is watching a play in which the action is natural. What began, then, as a powerful extension of drama into new areas of action and expression declined into a mannerism.[4]

Serious verse drama was gone as a really vital force before the two major trends that were to replace it had fully emerged. The first of these, and I believe the more significant, was a growing awareness of and response to European drama, which—in the work of Brecht, Adamov, Ionesco, Beckett and Sartre—had ultimately gone a long way to realizing in practise what the revival of verse drama had been seeking: the expansion of dramatic action and speech to include the widest possible kinds of human experience. Verse drama should not, however, be written off as a brave but futile experiment. As Dennis Welland reminds us,

The age of Osborne, Wesker, and Pinter might seem to call in question the very basic principles of verse drama by its almost despairing premise that the degree of communication possible between most people is so limited as to threaten the future of drama itself. Yet Kenneth Tynan once demonstrated convincingly the affinities between Pinter's dialogue and *Sweeney Agonistes*: it could be argued that Pinter's success would have been impossible without the Mercury Theater's poets. If they did nothing else, they made us aware that the rhythms of speech, repetitive or varying, fluid or staccato, can often communicate more than the prose meanings of the constituent words. . . . We should also remember that the poetry of poetic drama is not necessarily, or solely a verbal construct; it inheres in the structure of the play as a whole . . . .[5]

The assimilation of "Absurd Theater" was slow; indeed, the process is still neither final nor assured. In the early stages of this adjustment, another kind of theater appeared that was vociferous enough to make it appear to be the only important voice, one which has been called "Angry."

I The "Angry" Theater

In retrospect, it can be seen that the "Angry" dramatists were angry with what the theater was doing rather than with life around them. Their plays attacked nothing of real importance. J. R. Taylor, a sympathetic, even admiring critic, points out that in Shelagh Delaney's *A Taste of Honey*, "None of the characters look outward at life beyond the closed circle of the stage world; they all live for and in each other, and finally all the rest, even Helen, seem to exist only as incidentals in Jo's world, entering momentarily into her dream of life and vanishing when they have no further usefulness for it." And even of John Osborne's *Look Back in Anger*, the archetypal play of the genre, Taylor writes: "Faced at last with a really effective example of his own handiwork, Jimmy quails, and at last he and Alison are united again in their own idyllic dream world of bears and squirrels, content, perhaps, never to make it as human beings in the real world around."[6] These judgments are by a sympathetic critic who dates the new era in British drama from the production of *Look Back in Anger* (1956).

What John Osborne and the "Angries" did was to break through into the conventional theater by their sheer vitality, to encourage young dramatists to believe that plays could be produced, and to release a tremendous amount of energy and interest. Looking back at *Look Back in Anger* (1956) and *The Entertainer* (1957), John Arden's *Live Like Pigs* (1958), Delaney's *A Taste of Honey* (1958), and the plays of Arnold Wesker, we see the old romantic clichés about ordinary men and ordinary language used once more in plays that are, in fact, sentimental and conventional. Osborne is the most strident; Delaney, the one with a soft center; and Wesker, in his trilogy (*Chicken Soup with Barley* [1958], *Roots* [1959], and *I'm Talking About Jerusalem* [1960]), the most seriously committed of a group whose importance derived at first from their pseudosocial aims.

The problem of commitment in a writer has never been easy; and it hardly seems in question with Pinter: "He has shown himself almost morbidly sensitive to anything likely to compromise his independence or attach him to a group. He has voted only once (Labour) and that he regrets as a sentimental gesture; he invariably rejects attempts to enlist his support in any social or political movement; even when he was billed as a Royal Court Playwright in Sloane Square, he insisted on having his name removed." But the same *Observer* profile records two trials as a conscientious objector (in peacetime) which do not suggest a man unimpeded by a serious concern that approaches commitment. On the other hand, as John Mander has pointed out, *Look Back in Anger* is a vehement play, but it is also noncommittal! Commitment cannot only mean political involvement—any writer is obviously committed to a private quest for value in a valueless world: "Commitment is universal: the poet of subjectivity chooses to explore its inner rather than outer face."[7] Moreover, commitment must be found in the art, not the artist—a distinction the critic, faced with modern methods of publicity, finds harder to maintain: to confuse Jimmy Porter with his creator is plausible, and almost, one feels, inevitable; but to do so is still to fall into the biographical fallacy.

In short, the Angry Theater was not more real, more significant, nor more committed than the dramas of Pinter and N. F. Simpson. Indeed, G. E. Wellwarth may very well be right when he suggests that British national pride was roused by the success of Osborne's play and that *Look Back in Anger* is really a minutely accurate dissection of a perverse marriage in the style of Strindberg; but this observation does seem to locate the anger itself too peripherally. He is certainly right when, looking at what Hobson and Levin said about Wesker, he points out that Wesker's so-called working class is based on stock literary situations and caricature.[8] The Angry dramatists are, in fact, traditionalists; apart from conscious adaptations of Brechtian techniques, they did very little that was new in the way of using the theater differently. We are driven back, therefore, to their social aims to explain their importance. Jimmy Porter laments that there are no brave good causes left; yet these writers concern themselves with none of the important issues of the 1950's and 1960's. It may be true—as Bamber Gascoigne suggests—that the problems remaining for the Angries (the Bomb, the Cold War, world starvation) *were* too huge and too remote to be used in the theater;[9] but questions on the subjects are forced on us by the apparent aims of the drama. It is reasonable, then, to suggest that it was not *Look Back in Anger* in 1956 that initiated a new era, as Taylor claims, but the less-felt production in London in August, 1955, of Beckett's *Waiting for Godot*.

II *The "Absurd" Theater*

Samuel Beckett's *Waiting for Godot* introduced to the English stage, and English audience, the kind of theater that Martin Esslin has called "Theater of the Absurd," and which Wellwarth dates precisely from December 10, 1896, with the first performance of Alfred Jarry's *Ubu roi*. From Jarry's play followed the calculated insanity of 'Pataphysics, developed under Antonin Artaud into the spontaneous theater of "Cruelty" that reflects the condition of man faced with the unrelenting malignancy of the incomprehensible cosmic powers that govern him. The difference between Esslin and Wellwarth is worth noting: Esslin in *The Theater of the Absurd* (1961) deals only with that kind of theater and concentrates largely on the ideas behind it, its philosophical background, but Mr. Wellwarth is interested in the plays as things happening in a theater. The two books make a whole. But, as Wellwarth's title *The Theater of Protest and Paradox* implies, the Angry Theater finds a place in the latter as well as the Absurd and Cruel theaters, albeit that place is a comparatively low one. Wellwarth does not think much of protest unadorned with paradox. One should not dismiss Angry Theater in England too summarily, for it broke down a great number of theatrical barriers. Anger is essentially a dissolving emotion, and the plays of Anger were useful and important, just as verse drama was.

The New Theater

Absurd Theater does not even appear to have a social aim, however, and in the plays that Beckett produced—and, say, Ionesco and Adamov—the poetry is not in the language, which is kept deliberately flat and unpoetic, but resides in the action of the play, an action Esslin calls "Absurd." Basically this kind of theater seeks to express the feeling that the world cannot be explained or reduced to a system of values—and there are times when such a theater seems to be an invention of Mr. Esslin![10] It certainly leads to strange bedfellows. Grossvogel, in his book *Four Playwrights and a Postscript* (1962) uses Absurd Theater to link Brecht, Ionesco, Beckett, and Genet together, but Robert Brustein in *The Theater of Revolt* (1965) restricts the dominance of "existential revolt" to such diverse dramatists as Williams, Albee, Gelber, and Pinter. The whole idea behind such a theater is seriously challenged by Joseph Chiari in *Landmarks of Contemporary Drama* (1965) as being itself absurd.

III   Philosophy and Drama

Mr. Esslin relates contemporary drama to contemporary trends in philosophy. While the connections with Sartre and Existentialism are not inappropriate, they tend, perhaps, to be confusing —particularly as Existentialism itself seems to be an odd collection of writers and philosophers. Walter Kaufmann can link them only in terms of refusal: "The refusal to belong to any school of thought; the repudiation of the adequacy of any body of beliefs whatever, and especially of systems; and a marked dissatisfaction with traditional philosophy as superficial, academic, and remote from life—that is the heart of Existentialism."[11] They are, as Chiari remarks, a minority group.

The essential characteristics, reflected in the drama (whether Absurd or Cruel), are a preoccupation with failure, dread, and death. Such diverse figures as Kierkegaard, Dostoevsky, Nietzsche, Jaspers, Heidegger, Sartre, Rilke, and Kafka seem united in the perception of the absurdity of man's condition. Following in one direction derived from this perception (an important qualification, since Pascal reached the same conclusion about the human condition, but it moved him in the opposite direction), Camus' book *The Myth of Sisyphus* contains the statement of belief: an absurd hero is punished with a futile and hopeless labor. As well as Camus, Esslin quotes from Ionesco that "Absurd is that which is devoid of purpose. . . . Cut off from his religious, metaphysical, and transcendental roots, man is lost; all his actions become senseless, absurd, useless."[12] This feeling is echoed in another quotation from Ionesco: "A curtain, an impassable wall stands between me and the world, between me and myself; matter fills every corner, takes up all the space and its weight annihilates all freedom; the horizon closes in and the world becomes a stifling dungeon. Language breaks down in a different way and words drop like stones or dead bodies; I feel I am invaded by heavy forces, against which I can only fight a losing battle."[13]

Noticeably, the battle is one with both thought and the language to express that thought; and the most detailed treatment of the process and the malaise is *Nausea* by Jean-Paul Sartre (itself influenced, even to the sickness image, by Rilke's "The Notes of Malte Laurids Brigge"). In at least one play, *The Dwarfs*, Pinter comes very close to the problems of Roquentin in *Nausea*; and *The Homecoming* is a further consideration of this attitude toward life.

IV Nausea

Nausea, the diary of its hero, Roquentin, traces the growth of his sickness and the dissolution of the familiar world around him:

I looked anxiously around me: the present, nothing but the present. Furniture light and solid, rooted in its present, a table, a bed, a closet with a mirror and me. The true nature of the present revealed itself: it was what exists, and all that was not present did not exist. The past did not exist. Not at all. Not in things, not even in my thoughts. It is true that I had realised a long time ago that mine had escaped me. But until then I believed it had simply gone out of my range. For me the past was only a pensioning off: it was another way of existing, a state of vacation and inaction; each event, when it had played its part, put itself politely into a box and became an honorary event: we have so much difficulty imagining nothingness. Now I knew: these things are entirely what they appear to be and behind them . . . there is nothing.[14]

Dissolution becomes the descriptive word as the veneer of substance is stripped off:

And then all of a sudden, there it was, clear as day: existence had suddenly unveiled itself. It had lost the harmless look of an abstract category: it was the very paste of things, this root was kneaded into existence. Or rather the root, the park gates, the bench, the sparse grass, all that had vanished: the diversity of things, their individuality, were only an appearance, a veneer. This veneer had melted, leaving soft, monstrous masses, all in disorder—naked, in a frightful, obscene nakedness.[15]

From this state of affairs Roquentin arrives at truth:

And without formulating anything clearly, I understood that I had found the key to Existence, the key to my Nauseas, to my own life. In fact, all that I could grasp beyond that returns to this fundamental absurdity. Absurdity: another word; I struggle against words; down there I touched the thing. But I wanted to fix the absolute character of this absurdity here.[16]

As Iris Murdoch observes in her study of Sartre, Roquentin's metaphysical doubt is an old and familiar one: "The doubter sees the world of everyday reality as a fallen and bedraggled place, fallen out of the realm of being into the realm of existence. The circle does not exist; but neither does what is named as 'black' or 'table' or 'cold'! The relation of these words to their context of application is shifting and arbitrary. What *does* exist is brute and nameless, it escapes from the scheme of relations in which we imagine it to be rigidly enclosed, it escapes from language and science, it is more than and other than our description of it."[17] This is a realization that things which we recognise as stable, as having characteristics capable of being named and defined, do not in fact have these qualities unambiguously. That the labels are fixed by the observer, is, as Miss Murdoch suggests, one way of beginning philosophy. But is such a realization also a way of beginning drama? Esslin certainly sees it as a valuable key to recent drama—finds it, indeed, the impulse behind Absurd Theater: "The Theater of the Absurd . . . bravely faces up to the fact that for those to whom the world has lost its central explanation and meaning, it is no longer possible to accept art forms still based on the continuation of standards and concepts that have lost their validity; that is, the possibility of knowing laws of conduct and ultimate values, as deducible from a firm foundation of revealed certainty about the purpose of man in the universe."[18]

The Absurd dramatist is, therefore, uncommitted politically because he is engaged in a more subjective occupation (a judgment that must exclude both Sartre, whose politics are crucial, and Genet, whose commitments emerge ultimately as political). R. D. Smith writes: "A man must find himself without the support of groups, or labels, or slogans. Beckett, Ionesco and Pinter, engaged in finding or saving themselves, remove their characters from immediate social contexts."[19] But what may be true of Beckett or Ionesco is not true of Pinter, whose characters, for example, have very precise social contexts. It is true that Pinter is not politically committed. He is on record as saying:

I find most political thinking and terminology suspect, deficient. It seems to me a dramatist is entitled to portray the political confusion in a play if his characters naturally act in a political context, that is, if the political influences operating on them are more significant than any other considerations. But I object to the stage being used as a substitute for the soap box, where the author desires to make a direct statement at all costs, and forces his characters into fixed and artificial postures in order to achieve this. This is hardly fair on the characters. I don't care for the didactic or moralistic theater. In England I find this theater, on the whole, sentimental and unconvincing.[20]

This is probably a fair description of British theater. As far as Absurd philosophy in relation to drama is concerned, it remains true that the drama exercises the mind of an audience far larger, and even less united, than the minority of philosophers who preach it; and this should surely suggest that there is something more to the drama than a concept of the Absurd.

V *A Critical Catchphrase*

A character in James Saunder's Absurd drama *Next Time I'll Sing to You* remarks: "I'm not going to bandy existentialism with you"—an excellent resolution. As far as British drama is concerned, either experimental (Pinter, Simpson, or Saunders) or traditional (Osborne and Wesker), Existentialism seems to have afflicted critics rather than playwrights. In the introduction to the recent Penguin anthology, *Absurd Drama* (1965), Martin

Esslin has modified the position he adopted in his earlier book, *The Theater of the Absurd*. Admitting that the phrase has become much used and much abused, he still insists that critical concepts of this kind are useful when new conventions of art arise. Here, he suggests, were plays that flouted the criteria of the well-made play but still succeeded. The phrase "Theater of the Absurd" remains as a kind of "intellectual shorthand" to describe similarities and shared philosophical and artistic premises, whether conscious or unconscious; and it also helps to point to the central action of this kind of play, action no longer inherent in a plot (plots in Absurd dramas are usually quite static), but in the unfolding of a poetic image. Such images, he admits, lack clarity but strongly represent the loss of clear and well-defined systems of beliefs. Man finds himself faced with a frightening and illogical universe, in which the means of communication, language, is also suspect (and therefore the well-made play with its real conversation is also suspect). Esslin still rightly sees that philosophers and dramatists are responding to the same cultural and spiritual situation, although not with tears of despair but with the laughter of acceptance. This may be so, but the lumping of dramatists together is usually ill-advised.

Even if Beckett's *Waiting for Godot* and Pinter's *The Caretaker* were in the same world, which they are not, what help would this likeness give to dramatic criticism, whose function is to throw light on plays as plays, not as documents in eschatology? What we need desperately at this point is a critic like Dr. Johnson to kick the nearest stone. Thus, when Tennessee Williams uses a favorite quotation—"We are all of us sentenced to solitary confinement inside our own skins."—in the preface to *Cat on a Hot Tin Roof*, the ensuing play explores the remark—but plays cannot usually explicate criticism. There has been a loss of critical perspective about Absurdity. As F. N. Lees, writing about Beckett, has pointed out, the phrase has accuracy for Beckett only "as referring to the logician's *reductio ad absurdum*, a technique of demonstration, *not* a view of life."[21] In this sense, Pinter is also Absurd. When critics write of drama stripped for inaction (Beckett) or of the drama of anxiety (Ionesco), they are not merely generalising; they are also confusing technique with value. The fact that *The Bald Prima Donna* was written from a copy of the Assimil method of learning English is interesting history and illuminates that play, but it does not automatically confer any value on the play, which still has to satisfy an audience as a play—not as an experiment in adaptation.

VI *The Cult of Absurd Drama*

Absurd Theater is not, of course, a new phenomenon. As has been noted, Wellwarth traces it back to *Ubu roi* in 1896, while Esslin produces antecedents so extensive that one begins to feel that the whole of drama was merely a prelude to Absurd Theater. Eric Bentley in *The Playwright as Thinker* has shown how we can find the absurd in Wedekind, and the dream play in Maeterlinck, Andreyev or Strindberg. This kind of theater has always appeared in various forms, and the list of dramatists contains some unlikely names. Bertolt Brecht's *Baal* (1918) has a scene in which two characters, who have gambled with cards for their souls, wander on the stage, decide it is a good place to urinate, and do so—each seeking approval for the indecency. In Cocteau's *The Bridal Pair of the Eiffel Tower* (1921), two phonographs narrate crazy events. In e.e. cummings' *HIM* (1927), a character vomits in the hero's lap, and a woman carries a severed male organ on to the stage in a napkin. And *Sweeney Agonistes* (1927), had it been finished, would probably have been T. S. Eliot's contribution to the genre. Whether we call such drama Surrealism, Dadaism, or Absurd, in terms of what is happening in the theater, it is all of a piece. Only recently has it ceased to be a shocking cult and emerged to take its rightful place on the stage of the commercial theater. In this sense, the ideas behind it, or the techniques it uses, have corresponded with a wider audience than before.

Moreover, not so much the lack of logic as the madness of logic is behind it. Tynan, for once, seems to have missed the point: "Once having espoused the illogical, the irrelevant, the surreal, he [the Absurd dramatist] is committed; a single lapse into logic, relevance, or reality, and he is undone."[22] The kind of relentless logic behind absurdity is most evident in Pirandello, one of the forerunners of Beckett and Pinter, in plays like *Think It Over, Giacomino* (1916), *The Pleasure of Honesty* (1917), and *The Rules of the Game* (1918), a play that almost sets the pattern for this kind of drama.[23] In *The Rules of the Game*, a wife, estranged from her husband, tries to make it seem that she has been indecently approached by a young gallant who is a brilliant duelist. She hopes that her husband, in fulfilling his conventional obligations, will get killed and leave her free to enjoy life with her lover. To her surprise, her husband not only issues the challenge but names her lover as his second; but on the appointed day, he simply stays in bed. He has issued the challenge (a nominal function) because he is her husband (in his case, a nominal position); but her lover, as the *real* husband, has to fight the duel (the real obligation) and is killed. Here the husband logically applies the rules of the game.

Games of logic have been played frequently in contemporary drama—between husband and wife (Osborne's *Under Plain Cover*, Pinter's *The Lover*, or Albee's *Who's Afraid of Virginia Woolf*); between friends to pass the time (Beckett's *Waiting for Godot* or Pinter's *The Dumb Waiter*); or between strangers (Albee's *The Zoo Story*). Life is not so much absurd as it is a game that can be sinister, savage, pathetic, compassionate, and comic. Indeed, much of the stichomythic dialogue such a situation requires is noticeably music hall patter,[24] and this merging of the comic and tragic—though symptomatic of contemporary drama—is no new development. J. L. Styan produces antecedents that include the Mystery Plays, Euripides, Marlowe, Shakespeare, and Molière. But it is fair to point out that the mixture in these plays is less disturbing because it occurs in the context of an ethical conventionalism denied to contemporary drama. Even Dr. Johnson, in his famous *Preface to Shakespeare*, allows an appeal from the laws of Aristotle to nature. Contemporary drama is a kind of comedy that teases and troubles the audience while it makes it laugh.

VII   *Godot and His Children*

Pinter's only avowed influence was Beckett: ". . . there is no question that Beckett is a writer who I admire very much and have admired for a number of years. If Beckett's influence shows in my work that's all right with me. You don't write in a vacuum; you're bound to absorb and digest other writing and I admire Beckett's work so much that something of its texture might appear in my own."[25]

Wellwarth, calling Pinter "the dramatist of allusiveness," remarks, rather petulantly, that Pinter seems to have read all his secondary sources (for example, Beckett) but not the all-important primary source, Artaud—a curious obligation to put on any writer. In the statement just quoted by Pinter, he admits an admiration that may possibly have influenced—nothing more. It is an admission, however, that lends some justification to Esslin's calling Pinter one of the children of Godot in the article "Godot and His Children." Looking at a group of plays (Tardieu, *Qui est la* [1949], Adamov, *L'Invasion* [1950], and *Waiting for Godot* [1953]), Esslin sees them as plays that have abandoned beginning, middle, and end structures and that are remarkable for their use of dialogue "which is constantly exposed as an abortive attempt at communication" but which also reminds us of Chaplin or of Laurel and Hardy. Esslin naturally finds them based on Existentialist thought, showing general truths and ethical systems as mere illusions—and, in Beckett's work, as relentlessly pursuing the meaning of the phrase "I am myself." Esslin then applies this line of argument to Pinter: "Like Beckett, Pinter wants to communicate the mystery, the problematical nature, of man's situation in the world. However natural his dialogue, however naturalistic some of his situations may superficially appear, Pinter's plays are also basically images, almost allegories, of the human condition."[26] This split in Pinter is suggested in the *Observer* profile, September 15, 1963, the only biography so far, where he was seen as two people: "One is the dramatist who built up an imaginatively self-sufficient world out of fragments of common life often disregarded by other writers, and introduced a new type of theatrical poetry based on Cockney speech patterns. The other is a swarthy, vigorous ex-repertory actor with a tough, down-to-earth manner that would make him at home in a boxing gym or dockside pub." This distinction is as arbitrary in life as in literary criticism, but the former would be the allegorist, the latter, the naturalist.

Critics have placed Pinter in strange company, even in the narrow lists of British dramatists. Styan sees him as one of a group he calls the "comic ironists": "In England, at any rate, comic ironists like John Arden, David Campton, N. F. Simpson and, especially, Harold Pinter are now digging over the territory newly claimed. These dramatists practise a new illogicality, yet one pregnant with the logic of feeling that belongs to a subconscious world of tragicomedy. As in the novels of Franz Kafka and William Golding, the normal world of ordinary human relationships can suddenly become quick and sinister and even violent."[27] Blanket terms like "comic ironists" mean little, and lists merely cluster unconnected writers. The surprising omission in this list is Iris Murdoch, whose novels, owing as much as they do to Sartre and Ludwig Wittgenstein, fit more pertinently here than do, say, Golding's fables which, with the possible exception of *Free Fall*, are written as tight allegories rather than as discursive symbolism.

Styan describes Pinter as a light-heavyweight Beckett with a firmer sense of theater than N. F. Simpson has: "His audience is made to feel, through an exquisite friction of nightmare and normality, the earthly human need for security, recognition and acceptance. But society, by forcing us to conform, can destroy the very security we seek from it."[28] This quite customary conjunction of Simpson with Pinter is unfortunate because, if these dramatists are the nearest we have to *absurdistes* (Campton's work is limited and not widely known, while Arden has moved off in another direction), they do different things in their plays. Simpson has a splendid facility in a straightforward reduction of common human behavior to absurdity unattended by any larger implications; in their limited criticisms, Simpson's plays are much more the kind of social plays produced by Osborne and by Wesker rather than the plays of Beckett, Ionesco, or Pinter. Pinter's plays are held together by a dominant idea (hence the appropriateness of Esslin's phrase "almost allegories"), but Simpson's plays simply present the Absurd without any feeling that its presence springs from metaphysical doubts.[29]

Pinter can seem very Existential. In his article "Between the Lines," which appeared in *The Sunday Times* (March 4, 1962), he writes of the impossibility of verifying the past (even yesterday, or this morning!), the dangers of communication, and the impossibility of a final or definitive statement: "No statement I make, therefore, should be interpreted as final and definitive. One or two of them may sound final and definitive, but I won't regard them as such tomorrow and I wouldn't like you to do so today." But in reading the article, we are struck by Pinter's sense of humor more than anything else; such truth as such statements contain should be taken lightly.

VIII   A Theater of Despair?

There still remains the criticism applicable at any time to a drama of dreams and poetic images: if Absurd drama has been more profound than that of the social observers, and if it has struck at the heart and root of the matter, it has been too pessimistic—a view expressed by Sean O'Casey in "The Bald Primaqueera" (*Atlantic Monthly*, September, 1965). Put more positively by David Tutaev, how far can the theater get when it is all absurd?[30] Tutaev sees Absurd theater as part of a Romantic upsurge brought to the fore by great disasters; instead of making the best of man's experience, the Absurd dramatists have only seen the worst. They ignore, for example, the new advances and new materials of the world of science. Outside the shocking theater, man moves toward the stars, "defying existence not only with laughter, but with prayer, creating new theaters and new concepts as he escapes from that child of his age—the Theater of the Absurd." This statement seems rhetorical rather than critical; and Brecht as well as Beckett, Osborne as well as Pinter, would probably reject its implications.

Dramatists must surely confront, and go on confronting, neither the bomb nor the stars but a world of people who have to live with both. Pinter is concerned with humanity, love, necessity, and contingency—not in a lunar landscape but in the slum-dwelling next door. He does not, however, fall into the trap of explaining everything in terms of a poor environment. His stress on impoverished backgrounds in the early plays is itself relative, underlining the fact that all material assets have a fundamental paucity. Nor is the effect of his plays simply one of pessimism and despair. As Robert Bolt has observed: "I find—as in the plays of Pinter, too—things being said which are not absurd. I find for example in *Waiting for Godot* a kind of bitterness and a pain and a resentment expressed by this play and by these characters about the absurdity of life which seems to postulate that some reasonable expectation has not been met—otherwise, why the bitterness, why the pain, why the protest?"[31]

The New Theater

Pinter's plays are a commentary on that reasonable expectation and observation on its lack of fulfillment; they are suggestive of some, albeit often quite minimal, hope. For him, the plays are their own justification; and hope for the system in which they exist is suggested because they do exist:

No, I'm not committed as a writer, in the usual sense of the term, either religiously or politically. And I'm not conscious of any particular social function. I write because I want to write. I don't see any placards on myself, and I don't carry any banners. Ultimately I distrust any definitive labels. As far as the state of the theater is concerned, I'm as conscious as anyone else of the flaws of procedure, of taste, of the general setup in management, and I think things will go on more or less as they are for some considerable time. But it seems to me that there has been a certain development in one channel or another in the past three years. *The Caretaker* wouldn't have been put on, and certainly wouldn't have run, before 1957. The old categories of comedy and tragedy and farce are irrelevant, and the fact that managers seem to have realized that is one of the favorable changes. But writing for the stage is the most difficult thing of all, whatever the system. I find it more difficult the more I think about it.[32]

CHAPTER 2

Comedies of Menace

THE TITLE of this chapter is more than a witty summary; it points to a mixture of genres. As J. L. Styan has pointed out, the audience of a contemporary drama often suffers the peculiar misery of changing sides during the action. We find here a comedy that frightens and causes pain. And because Pinter's development of this kind of play, like most writer's work, is a matter of discovery in each play of an extension to be used in the next—accumulating intensity by the use and reuse of certain ideas, images, and situations—it is more than simple chronology that makes his early work the best place to begin. There could be no better way of tracing that development than by starting with Pinter's early plays, written in 1957 and subsequently performed with little initial success: *The Room, The Birthday Party,* and *The Dumb Waiter.*

In an article significantly called "Writing for Myself," Pinter has traced his own career in response to the question "What kind of audience do you have in mind?" Pinter believes that if one has a message to give, one becomes a political or religious teacher, but not a dramatist. Writing, for him, is a very personal thing, done for his own benefit: "Firstly and finally, and all along the line you write because there's something you *want* to write, *have* to write. For yourself."[1] Pinter then sketches his early career as an actor for about nine years (under the name of David Baron) and the obvious influence this experience had on his plays—an influence, that is to say, on the construction and dialogue of his plays. All the time he was acting, he was writing, not plays, but poems and short prose pieces. Many of these were, however, in dialogue form; this prepared the way for his revue sketches, in particular, and for his plays, in general. He also, surprisingly, wrote a novel based on part of his youth in Hackney. It was never published but was later developed into the play *The Dwarfs.* Some of his poems were published, particularly in

Poetry London, where they are sometimes ascribed to a Harold Pinta.[2]

It is difficult to judge these poems uninfluenced by Pinter's later success in using words as a dramatist; it is difficult, that is, not to read into them an importance they might not in themselves possess. Naturally, because of his later career, they are both important and interesting. They have something of the exuberance of Dylan Thomas, but they are mainly concerned with life in the city, as in "New Year in the Midlands," published in November, 1950:

Now here again she blows, landlady of lumping
Fellows between the boards.
Singing "O Celestial Light," while
Like a T-square on the
Flood swings her wooden leg.
This is the shine, the powder and blood and here am I,
Straddled, exile always in one Whitbread Ale town,
Or such.
Where we went to the yellow pub, cramped in an alley bin,
A shoot from the market,
And found the thin Luke of a queer, whose pale
Deliberate eyes, raincoat, Victorian,
Sap the answer in the palm.
All the crush, camp, burble and beer
Of this New Year's Night; the psalm derided;
The black little crab women with the long
Eyes, lisp and claw in a can of chockfull stuff.
I am rucked in the heat of treading; the wellrolled
Sailor boys soon rocked to sleep, whose ferret fig
So calms the coin of a day's fever.
Now in this quaver of a roisty bar, the wansome lady
I blust and stir,
Who pouts the bristle of a sprouting fag—
Sprinkled and diced in these Midland lights
Are Freda the whimping glassy bawd, and your spluttered guide,
Blessed with ambrosial bitter weed.—Watch
How luminous hands
Unpin the town's genitals—
Young men and old
With the beetle glance,
The crawing brass whores, the clamping
Red shirted boy, ragefull, thudding his cage.

Apart from the exuberant use of language, which Pinter has never lost but has learned to control, the theme, even here, is loneliness, exile, and the feverish coming together bitterly achieved in drink or sex on a New Year's Eve.

In 1957, Pinter turned, however, to writing plays, plays that he has always claimed are not planned in advance, but which grow imaginatively out of a situation in his mind:

I went into a room one day and saw a couple of people in it. This stuck with me for some time afterwards, and I felt that the only way I could give it expression and get it off my mind was dramatically. I started off with this picture of two people and let them carry on from there. It wasn't a deliberate switch from one kind of writing to another. It was quite a natural movement. A friend of mine, Henry Woolf, produced the result—*The Room*—at Bristol University, and a few months later in January 1958 it was included—in a different production—in the festival of University drama. Michael Codron heard about the play and wrote to me at once to ask if I had a full-length play. I had just finished *The Birthday Party*. . . .

The descriptive name—"Comedies of Menace"—that these plays have acquired first appeared as the subtitle of a play in four "glimpses" by David Campton called *The Lunatic View* (1957). Campton's play was offered to an England not habituated as yet to Ionesco, to an England indeed in which Pinter and Simpson would have to wait two or three years before any sort of receptive public emerged. Unlike most *absurdistes*, Campton explicitly devoted the Absurd theater to social comment: "To my mind the Theater of the Absurd is a weapon against complacency (which spreads like a malignant fungus). The weapon of complacency is the pigeon-hole. Pigeon-hole an idea, and it becomes harmless. (We have a clean bomb.) It is difficult to be complacent when the roots of one's existence are shaken, which is what the Absurd at its best does. Of course, now, having been given a name, the Theater of the Absurd is in danger of being popped into a pigeon-hole itself. . . ."[3]

In Campton's "sick" comedies, the menace is clear enough, but in Pinter's plays, the potency of menace derives from an inability to define its source or reason even though it is all-pervasive. If it can be categorized, it is simply the constant threat to the individual personality, a vague enough category to keep it alive. Moreover, Pinter's plays escape a possible objection to *Waiting for Godot,* in which the menace is weakened by a symbolic landscape—a rather unearthly setting with vaguely cosmic implications. This comparison is only to suggest, of course, that Pinter is not Beckett and is doing something else. Pinter's terror and menace are greater because they exist in the house next door. Taylor has suggested that Pinter, as an East End Jew, grew up during the war, when menace was a familiar pattern. But the "Tempo" program about his adolescence in Hackney put out on commercial television in September, 1965, records an atmosphere of violence in Hackney that Pinter explicitly does not attribute to his Jewishness. As Edwin Muir wrote of Kafka, Pinter opens up one of the ordinary doors through which we enter the universal situation.[4] On the surface, there is nothing extraordinary about the room that gives Pinter's first play its title, locale, and situation.

I The Room

This first play, *The Room,* drew an admiring notice from Harold Hobson on its performance at Bristol University (which in turn prompted the calamitous first London performance of *The Birthday Party,* killed immediately by an almost unanimously abusive press). As the title suggests, *The Room* is a compressionistic play rather than an epic (that is, its influences are Beckett's *Endgame,* Ionesco's *The Chairs,* Sartre's *Huis Clos,* and Chekhov rather than Brecht). Written in four days, it is about two people in a room: "Two people in a room—I am dealing a great deal of the time with this image of two people in a room. The curtain goes up on the stage and I see it as a very potent question: What is going to happen to these two people in the room? Is someone going to open the door and come in?"[5] But of what exactly they are afraid, we never learn: we feel an unspecified menace.[6]

The play is not, finally, successful. Martin Esslin puts his finger on its main fault: the use of melodramatic devices entirely out of keeping with the subtly composed terrors of the beginning of the play.[7] Yet Esslin himself interprets the play symbolically: the room becomes an image of the small area of light and warmth that our consciousness, the fact that we exist, opens up in the vast ocean of nothingness from which we gradually emerge after birth and into which we sink again when we die.[8] In other words, the room is a Naturalistic equivalent of Beckett's dustbins, urns, and sacks. But it is difficult to decide whether or not this equivalence is suggested by the wisdom of hindsight, stimulated by the ideas explored in later plays. In this play more than ever, as Clifford Leech astutely remarks, are we "conscious of being invited to look for allegory and yet not sufficiently impelled to conduct the search."[9] This dilemma partly stems from the language of the play. When Pinter was asked whether or not his creative imagination was more visual than verbal, he replied: "I see things pretty clearly, certainly, but I am continually surprised by what I see and by what suddenly happens in the play while I am writing it. I do not know, however, that the visual is more important to me than the verbal, because I am pretty well obsessed with words when they get going. It is a matter of tying the words to the image of the character standing on the stage. The two things go very closely together."[10] Dramatists like Pinter and Simpson have discovered the language of cliché as a stage device, revealing to audiences that an apparently meticulous reproduction of "real" conversation produces a result more striking in many ways than either verse or attempted Naturalism. Most real conversation, as overheard in a restaurant or on a bus, is frankly repetitive, incoherent, elliptical, and ungrammatical. A controlled transcription of this language produces dialogue for the theater of the Absurd: controlled, because a transcription, in order to be useful, must be guided by the dramatist as a stream-of-consciousness technique is guided by the novelist; from it certain patterns emerge.

The Room contains the style, themes, and setting for Pinter's work up to and including *The Caretaker*. It is important to recognize at this stage that the style is itself part of the theme of the play: "His characters do not use language to show that language doesn't work; they use it as a cover for their fear and loneliness. They move each in his separate prison—the old man selling evening newspapers, the landlady who gives Petey his cornflakes."[11] The world of these people is first seen and felt in *The Room,* where we find a ruthless and strategic mimicry of irrelevancy, incoherence, and taciturnity—the inability and the unwillingness to communicate—of everyday life and speech. The action is apparently unmotivated and goes unexplained.

In a shabby room in a large house, Rose, a woman of 60, is

fussing over her husband, Bert, a man of 50, a van driver, who appears to be rather simple-minded but who never speaks to her, not even to reply to her rambling monologue on the virtues of the room they live in. Outside this room the weather is cold and wintry (the second line of the play, referring to the weather, is ominously "It's murder"). Pinter frequently uses the weather outside to emphasize the protective envelope or womb that the room appears to form around the characters. Rose's almost motherly solicitude for Bert is *partly* justified by the fact, suggested later in the play, that he has been ill; and her obsessive clinging to such a shabby place is *partly* explained by the fact, suggested later, that they have just moved into the area. However, neither of these facts can be taken as necessarily true or false. Like all statements of fact in Pinter, they are capable of neither proof nor denial. This room for Rose is comfortable, representing, as it does, her only security; and it is just right for her—it is not in the basement (which is cold and damp) nor too far up (if there are rooms higher up). Also nobody bothers them:

This is a good room. You've got a chance in a place like this. I look after you, don't I, Bert? Like when they offered us the basement here I said no straight off. I knew that'd be no good. The ceiling right on top of you. No, you've got a window here, you can move yourself, you can come home at night, if you have to go out, you can do your job, you can come home, you're all right. And I'm here. You stand a chance.[12]

Pinter's plays are simply about people bothering people who want to keep to themselves. In his article "Between the Lines," Pinter suggested that failure to communicate was probably the wrong description of what happens in life and in his plays: "I think that we communicate only too well, in our silence, in what is unsaid, and that what takes place is continual evasion, desperate rearguard attempts to keep ourselves to ourselves. Communication is too alarming." And he is elsewhere quoted as saying that communication is a very fearful matter.

The first intruder is the landlord, Mr. Kidd, who arrives, talks, but does not communicate. He and Rose do, however, confirm each other's opinion that this room is the best in the house —the downstairs is damp; upstairs, the rain comes in. Even Mr. Kidd seems vague about the scope and extent of the house—

which room was what in the past—and even about his parentage, since he cannot decide whether his mother was or was not a Jewess. Although he suggests that the house is full at the moment, he also says that he can take his pick of the rooms for his own bedroom. His conversation tells Rose nothing and confuses us; it is shifty and uneasy. When he leaves, he is followed a little later by the silent Bert. Rose begins to tidy up. Opening the door to empty the garbage can, she finds a young couple groping about on the landing in the dark and invites them in. Clarissa and Toddy Sands, who are looking for a room, have been told that there is one vacant in the house, but they have been unable to find the landlord or to explore the house, which is in darkness. As a married couple (presumably), they, too, seem on edge with each other; indeed, the verbal battles between these two introduce comedy into the play, although beneath the comedy is the question of what causes the tensions, and also the menace of differences—they, for example, know the landlord by another name. As they bicker over whether Toddy should or should not sit down, whether Clarissa did or did not see a star, our laughter is tinged with a sense of the ominous. When Toddy accidentally does sit down, Clarissa pounces:

Mrs. Sands: You're sitting down.
Mr. Sands (*jumping up*): Who is?
Mrs. Sands: You were.
Mr. Sands: Don't be silly. I perched.
Mrs. Sands: I saw you sit down.
Mr. Sands: You did not see me sit down because I did not sit bloody well down. I perched!
Mrs Sands: Do you think I can't perceive when someone's sitting down?
Mr. Sands: Perceive! That's all you do. Perceive.
Mrs. Sands: You could do with a bit more of that instead of all that tripe you get up to.
Mr. Sands: You don't mind some of that tripe!
Mrs. Sands: You take after your uncle, that's who you take after!
Mr. Sands: And who do you take after?
Mrs. Sands (*rising*): I didn't bring you into the world.
Mr. Sands: You didn't what?
Mrs. Sands: I said, I didn't bring you into the world.
Mr. Sands: Well, who did then? That's what I want to know. Who did? Who did bring me into the world?[13]

Irrelevant and inconsequential, this dialogue yet has the menaces of sex and religion in it. On the plot level, these interchanges amusingly delay the information that the frightened Rose desperately wants to have (about which room *is* vacant) and fears to have: namely, that a man sitting in the dark in the basement has said that Room Seven, Rose's room, is vacant. Rose is naturally apprehensive of losing her room (warmth, light, and security) and of being driven out into the rest of the house, which she neither understands nor likes. She gets rid of the Sandses, and Mr. Kidd bursts in again. But, as Rose tries to question him about her room and what the Sandses have told her (that it is to let), he, too, tries to tell her something, something he can only tell her when Bert is away. This information, again, *partly* explains the inconsequential nature of his first visit but raises more questions in doing so (namely, why *has* Bert to be out of the house before he can tell her?). There is, he says, a man in the basement who is waiting to see her, who will not go away without seeing her, and who just sits there waiting, not even willing to play a game of chess to pass the time. Rose is finally convinced that she must see this stranger by the alarming thought that he might come while Bert was there (again why?), so, she tells Mr. Kidd to send him up quickly. A blind Negro enters (which *partly* explains why he was sitting in the dark) who says his name is Riley and whom Rose immediately attacks for upsetting the landlord. But her speech contains one or two curious phrases —"you're all deaf, dumb and blind, *the lot of you*"; "oh, these *customers*" (italics mine)—that are obscure. And why does Rose deny that his name is Riley if she does not know him? Her harangue culminates in a denial that is also a request:

ROSE: You've got what? How could you have a message for me, Mister Riley, when I don't know you and nobody knows I'm here and I don't know nobody anyway. You think I'm an easy touch, don't you? Well, why don't you give it up as a bad job? Get off out of it. I've had enough of this. You're not only a nut, you're a blind nut and you can get out the way you came. *Pause.*
What message? Who have you got a message from? Who?
RILEY: Your father wants you to come home.[14]

The Negro repeats the message, calling her "Sal"—a name she does not deny; indeed, since she says "Don't call me that," she

almost admits to it. As she is feeling his face with her fingers
(itself the action of a blind person rather than of a seeing one),
Bert returns. He describes, in one short, violent speech, his
furious drive back, how the one car that got in his way got
"bumped," and how the van (which is feminine) goes well with
him. Then he sits down and looks at the Negro for a few minutes. Suddenly he throws the Negro on the floor with the single
word: "Lice." Then Bert beats him to death against the gas stove
while Rose screams and announces that she is blind.

II *Symbolism in* The Room

It is this Negro who causes most trouble in the play: "The
Negro may symbolize death, the woman's past, or some hidden
guilt complex—probably the latter, since she is struck blind when
her husband beats the Negro. But there is no hint as to what his
function really is nor as to why the husband beats him so savagely. He is simply an emissary from the outside who has succeeded
in breaking into the circle of light. As a result, the womb is
broken, and the dwellers are cast out from the light into the
darkness."[15] It is possible to explain certain puzzles (a blind man
sits in the dark) or to provide motives (Sal has become Rose—as
Sal, she lead the sort of life with other men that would make
Bert excessively jealous) but always uncertainly (Rose is, after
all, 60!). And is her father from whom the message comes the
kind of father we find in a play by T. S. Eliot? Intruders are
repelled, violently; but what value has a room which seems
overprotective, even stifling? Are the intruders good or bad or
neither? What meaning does the constant imagery of warmth/
cold, light/dark suggest in the play? The melodrama of the end
is undeniably unfortunate, and not least in its crude pseudo-
symbolism; but the basic Pinter device (as it develops in the
later plays) of linguistic contradictions, in which statements are
given importance until doubt is thrown on them by another or
even the same character, appears. As J. R. Taylor puts it: "The
technique of casting doubt upon everything by matching each
apparently clear and unequivocal statement with an equally
clear and unequivocal statement of its contrary . . . is one which
we shall find used constantly in Pinter's plays to create an air of
mystery and uncertainty."[16]

The situations themselves are simple and basic, and the language, in itself, is a fairly accurate reproduction of ordinary conversation in everyday circumstances, although there is a higher content of metaphorical significance than is usual. And yet ultimately, the question the plays ask is: can we ever know the truth about anybody or anything? Is there, in fact, an absolute truth to be known? Part of the weakness of *The Room*, as Taylor suggests, is that the suppression of motives often seems to be merely an arbitrary device. But in the later plays, it would be more accurate to say that no one, even one who acts, can know what precisely impels action. In *The Room* it is not so much, we feel, that motives are unknowable as that the author will not let us know them. The play remains, however, a good piece of theater. The final explosion occurs so rapidly and so unexpectedly that the audience is left stunned, which is not a bad conclusion to a play.

III   *Criticism of* The Room

The Room has evoked some odd critical responses, particularly from those critics who have tried to find an allegory. Miss Ruby Cohn, for example, sees the basic theme of Pinter's plays as Man versus System; hence, Rose is Bert's victim: "Of the rival claimants for Rose, Riley and Bert, the latter bludgeons his way to triumph. Bert's role as villain explodes climactically, for it is Riley who first appears to menace Rose. But silence, connubial demands, and a van (female in Bert's lines) are victorious over the blind Negro father-surrogate."[17] But it could be suggested that the first menace is really life itself; the second, Bert's illness; the third, a whimsical and forgetful landlord; the fourth, the Sandses; the fifth, a visitor who menaces because of a past Rose would presumably prefer to forget. Life for Rose, as for all of us, is full of menace. The claims of Riley and Bert are not exactly the same, and a great deal of the violence generated toward the end of the play seems to rest upon Riley's color (Mr. Pinter, a Jew, uses Jews in his later plays, but here, of course, the Negro is useful to contain the implications of dark and light). And, of course, vans in English are usually feminine, so we need not read too much into that.

J. T. Boulton concentrates on the mother/son + husband relationship between Rose and Bert (echoed slightly in the Clarissa/ Toddy Sands argument about who brought him into the world):

The whole scene, linguistically and visually, suggests a mother-son relationship rather than wife-husband. The pathos springs from the sense of loneliness: Bert is isolated by his own silence, Rose is herself isolated within the emotional world of her own creation. When Riley, the blind Negro, appears at the end of the play to threaten this world with a message purporting to be from her father and requesting her to return "home," Rose spurns him with an almost frenzied determination. We see Rose passionately trying to safeguard the world she has built up to hide her solitariness; her passion is translated into terms of physical violence by Bert, who recognizes the threat represented by the intruding Negro; and the blindness transferred from Riley to Rose further emphasizes her isolation which is now complete. She has rejected the demands made on her by family affection (whether we regard this as her own particular family or the larger human family of society); to respond to such demands would require active involvement in the affairs of others; Rose prefers to take refuge behind the flimsy emotional barrier she has laboriously erected against the outside world.[18]

But it must be remembered that Bert is 50 and Rose 60—therefore their relationship can hardly be that of young lovers—while the Grand Guignol touch of a blind Negro, in an English play at any rate, if it means anything at all, must mean something more Gothic than simply the demands of society. Apart from these reservations, such an interpretation has the virtue of plausibility and the vice of pretentiousness. For those who want to find motives in the play (and in one sense it shows that motives are impossible), it is a simple matter to translate it to the same background as that of Sartre's *The Respectful Prostitute*, the Deep South, where what Rose fears is the discovery that she has black blood. However, such a translation makes nonsense of the play, spoils the comedy, removes the mystery of the menace, and robs the play of its Englishness.

IV   The Birthday Party

The Birthday Party, also written in 1957, was produced as an immediate consequence of the Bristol production of *The Room*. First presented at the Arts Theatre in Cambridge and subsequently at the Lyric in Hammersmith, it was disastrously unsuccessful. The story of Pinter's growth as a dramatist is very much the story of the education of critics and audiences about his particular style. This necessity is stressed in Irving Wardle's almost uniquely sympathetic review in *Encore*, which deserves full quotation:

Nowadays there are two ways of saying you don't understand a play: the first is to bowl it out with the word "obscurity," once so popular in poetry reviews; the second way is to say that the seminal influence of Ionesco can be detected.

Mr. Pinter received the full treatment. As well as standing for x in the formulae above, he was described as inferior N. F. Simpson, a lagging surrealist, and as the equal of Henry James. Remembering James's melancholy affair with the theater this last one carries a nasty sting; and within a couple of days of receiving it, *The Birthday Party* was over.

The comparison with James is quite baffling. Far from being a cautious verbal artist struggling to "throw away cargo to save the ship," Mr. Pinter has no difficulty in putting theatrical requirements first. No matter what you may think of the contents, the ship is afloat. And it is his very instinct for what will work in the theater that has prompted hostility. One character in *The Birthday Party*, for instance, is given to tearing up newspapers: we are not told why. But the spectacle of John Stratton, as the inflammable McCann, holding his breath while rapt in the task of tearing each strip of paper to the same width, took on a malevolent power perfectly in key with the play and requiring no explanation. This device is an extreme example of the playwright's habit of introducing an intrinsically theatrical idea and letting it find its own road back towards common sense. Mr. Pinter's way is the opposite of setting out deliberately to embody a theme in action.

All the same a theme does emerge, closely resembling that of *The Iceman Cometh*: the play demonstrates that a man who has withdrawn to protect his illusions is not going to be helped by being propelled into the outer world. Stanley, the man in question, is an obese, shambling, unpresentable creature who has moved into a dilapidated seaside boarding house where, as the only guest, he is able to lord it over his adoring landlady and gain recognition as a concert pianist of superhuman accomplishment. But even in this protected atmosphere there are menacing intrusions: he cannot banish the memory of arriving to give a recital and finding the hall locked up; there are enemies. And when they arrive—in the persons of a suspiciously fluent

Jew and his Irish henchman—they seem as much furies emerging from Stanley's night thoughts as physical creatures. His downfall is swift. Scrubbed, shaved, hoisted out of his shapeless trousers, and stuffed into a morning suit he is led away at the end in a catatonic trance.[19]

This review misses very little about the play or its theatrical context. The one point it does miss is important, as we shall suggest; but, amid criticism that was banal and uncomprehending, Mr. Wardle had at least listened to the play. He could, of course, have compared it more fruitfully, as Jacqueline Hoefer does, with John Whiting's *Saint's Day*: both plays, about a birthday party, have the theme of an alienated artist opposed to society, an artist accused of social betrayal for having left the organization; but, as Miss Hoefer remarks, the Whiting play has the urgency of alarm, while *The Birthday Party* has the finality of a post mortem in which the artist has lost his function before the play begins.[20]

The Birthday Party opens with breakfast at the Boles's. Meg and Petey Boles live in a run-down boarding house at a seaside resort (Petey is apparently a deck-chair attendant), and they have only one guest, Stanley. The opening scene is reminiscent of both *The Room* (Meg mothers Petey and hates going out, for example) and *The Dumb Waiter* (which also starts with items read from the newspaper). From the apparent inconsequentiality of news items read out by Petey—that Lady Mary Splatt has had a baby, a girl—emerges the possible fact that Meg needs a son and that the lodger, Stanley, fulfills that role as well as that of a young lover. Petey announces the possible arrival of two new guests, and Meg goes up to waken Stanley—a noisy game from which she appears panting and rearranging her hair. Stanley enters, "unshaven, in his pyjama jacket and wearing glasses." Over breakfast he teases Meg with words and innuendo—calling her fried bread "succulent," a word she is certain is an improper comment on herself. Stanley was, apparently, a great concert pianist who was stopped in his career by "them." He is alarmed and unbelieving when told that two guests are coming. He pretends, with ironic cruelty, that they are coming to cart Meg away in a wheelbarrow.

A young girl, Lulu, who comes in with a mysterious parcel,

tries to get Stanley to pull himself together and to come out with her. After she has left, he goes into the kitchen to wash himself and hides there, observing the arrival of the two new guests, Nathaniel Goldberg and Dermot McCann, who are looking for a particular place to do a specific job. These two strangers remind us of the two gunmen in *The Dumb Waiter*, particularly in that McCann, the younger of the two strangers, feels that the organization they represent no longer trusts him—with some reason it appears, for he is questioning its orders. He is, after much pressing, formally answered by Goldberg, in a "quiet, fluent, official tone":

GOLDBERG: The main issue is a singular issue and quite distinct from your previous work. Certain elements, however, might well approximate in points of procedure to some of your other activities. All is dependent on the attitude of our subject. At all events, McCann, I can assure you that the assignment will be carried out and the mission accomplished with no excessive aggravation to you or myself. Satisfied?
McCANN: Sure. Thank you, Nat.[21]

When Meg joins them, she lets slip that it is Stanley's birthday, and Goldberg immediately insists that they must have a party in spite of Stanley's protestations that it is not really his birthday. Stanley seems a little depressed after the strangers have gone upstairs, and to cheer him up, Meg gives him the mysterious parcel, his birthday present. In it is a toy drum (to replace his piano!), and the first act ends with Stanley marching round the room beating this drum—his beat growing more and more savage until, in the end, he is completely and frighteningly out of control.

Act Two opens with McCann alone, tearing a newspaper into five strips, slowly and painstakingly—surely a reasonable dramatization of the insecurity betrayed in Act One.[22] Stanley comes in and tries to discover what connections McCann and Goldberg have in common, what associations the two strangers have with his previous life in either Basingstoke or Ireland. He tries to get rid of them by saying there is no room; and, after a little "game" of sitting down and standing up, he finds himself being questioned. McCann and Goldberg begin an interrogation that takes the form of a kind of litany in which serious and frivolous charges are balanced in the syntax of denunciation:

GOLDBERG: Where is your lechery leading you?
MCCANN: You'll pay for this.
GOLDBERG: You stuff yourself with dry toast.
MCCANN: You contaminate womankind.
GOLDBERG: Why don't you pay the rent?
MCCANN: Mother defiler!
GOLDBERG: Why do you pick your nose?
MCCANN: I demand justice!
GOLDBERG: What's your trade?
MCCANN: What about Ireland?
GOLDBERG: What's your trade?
STANLEY: I play the piano.
GOLDBERG: How many fingers do you use?
STANLEY: No hands!
GOLDBERG: No society would touch you. Not even a building society.
MCCANN: You're a traitor to the cloth.
GOLDBERG: What do you use for pyjamas?
STANLEY: Nothing.
GOLDBERG: You verminate the sheet of your birth.
MCCANN: What about the Albigensenist heresy?
GOLDBERG: Who watered the wicket in Melbourne?
MCCANN: What about the blessed Oliver Plunkett?
GOLDBERG: Speak up Webber. Why did the chicken cross the road?[23]

The potential violence and ugliness in this scene is prevented only by the arrival of Meg in her party dress beating Stanley's drum. A party follows whose central event is a speech by Goldberg (echoing Meg's evocation of her childhood pink room with its night light) in which he regrets the loss of love, which was so comfortably present in the nursery days:

"How can I put it to you? We all wander on our tod through this world. It's a lonely pillow to kip on."[24]

At first Stanley does not participate in his birthday party; but, when Lulu suggests a game of blindman's buff, he is drawn in. At this point, the reader of both plays will detect echoes of *The Room*: there is even a song about Reilly. As the blindfolded Stanley picks his way across the room (McCann removes his spectacles first and breaks them quietly), McCann pushes the drum in his way, and Stanley crashes his foot through it. There is great merriment until he catches Meg and tries to strangle her. At this point all the lights go out. In the ensuing melee, McCann drops the flashlight (Goldberg's orders were apparently that Stanley should be kept spotlighted all the time), and, when it is found, Lulu "is lying spread-eagled on the table, Stanley bent over her." When Goldberg and McCann bear down upon him with the light, he retreats giggling to the wall.

The third act opens once more with breakfast at the Boles's. Meg and Petey, who could not attend the party, discuss the party and Stanley's illness. His friends are looking after him, and Goldberg's large car waits outside to take him away. Stanley has had some sort of breakdown. Petey offers to help—to get a doctor or to find tape to repair the broken glasses; but such offers are brushed aside by the smoothly professional Goldberg. However, when McCann comes down from Stanley's room, he seems upset and begins to tear the newspaper rapidly into strips. In the tension this action seems to generate, and because McCann inadvertently calls Goldberg "Simey," a quarrel breaks out. The fight between Goldberg and McCann is terminated by Goldberg's statement of faith: never change and always do what you are told:

> Because I believe that the world . . . (*Vacant.*) . . . .
> Because I believe that the world . . . (*Desperate.*) . . . .
> BECAUSE I BELIEVE THAT THE WORLD . . . (*Lost.*) . . . .[25]

This uneasiness is also physical. Even Goldberg has to have a kind of medical check-up and the "kiss-of-life" treatment to reassure himself that he is in perfect condition.[26]

Lulu arrives, but her attempted seduction seems less comic when she learns that Goldberg is leaving:

> LULU: You're leaving?
> GOLDBERG: Today.
> LULU (*with growing anger*): You used me for a night. A passing fancy.
> GOLDBERG: Who used who?
> LULU: You made use of me by cunning when my defences were down.
> GOLDBERG: Who took them down?
> LULU: That's what you did. You quenched your ugly thirst. You took advantage of me when I was overwrought. I wouldn't do those things again, not even for a Sultan!

GOLDBERG: One night doesn't make a harem.

LULU: You taught me things a girl shouldn't know before she's been married at least three times!

GOLDBERG: Now you're a jump ahead! What are you complaining about?[27]

The return of McCann, who has gone up to get Stanley ready, turns this game into another potential interrogation. But when Lulu is ordered to confess, she wisely leaves. Stanley is brought in transformed: striped trousers, black jacket, white collar, carrying a bowler hat and his broken glasses. He is clean, neat, and shaven, and the two men begin to woo him with relish. But Stanley is dumb and the litany of promises only produces a wordless wail. Petey makes one last attempt to intervene, but on being invited to go along, he, too, retreats, and the two men take Stanley away to "Monty." The play closes with Meg still unaware that Stanley has gone.

V   *The Meaning of* The Birthday Party

Goldberg and McCann promise Stanley a new birth:

GOLDBERG: We'll make a man of you.
McCANN: And a woman.
GOLDBERG: You'll be reoriented.
McCANN: You'll be rich.
GOLDBERG: You'll be adjusted.
McCANN: You'll be our pride and joy.
GOLDBERG: You'll be a mensch.
McCANN: You'll be a success.
GOLDBERG: You'll be integrated.
McCANN: You'll give orders.
GOLDBERG: You'll make decisions.[28]

But, when Petey opens his newspaper at the end of the play, five carefully torn strips of newspaper remind us of one thing Mr. Wardle missed—something that explains why these agents, although so humanly lecherous, like officials in Kafka, cannot stop being mysterious. As Clifford Leech observes, Goldberg and McCann, squalid, uncertain, whimsical, and cruel agents of a power Stanley has somehow disobeyed, are the more frightening because they themselves are ill at ease. At the end of the play, Petey's guilt is our own.[29]

Mention of Kafka is frequent when dealing with modern drama. To a Polish critic, Gregorz Sinko, Kafka is the obvious key to an interpretation of Pinter's work. As Sinko points out, in *The Birthday Party* we see the destruction of the victim from the victim's own point of view: "One feels like saying that the two executioners, Goldberg and McCann, stand for all the principles of state and social conformism. Goldberg refers to his 'job' in a typically Kafka-esque official language which deprives the crime of all sense and reality." And of his removal: "Maybe Stanley will meet his death there or maybe he will only receive a conformist brainwashing after which he is promised . . . many other gifts of civilisation. . . ."[30] Not exactly fusing with this view is another layer concerning the illusions of Meg as queen of the ball, reminiscent of a Naturalistic play by Tennessee Williams. Such an interpretation seems to me reasonably satisfactory when made by a Polish critic for whom the world of Kafka is not entirely fictional; but it is less so in the context of an English seaside resort. Too strongly the cliché asserts itself: it couldn't happen here. And, indeed, it is the Naturalistic surface of the play that is very strong.

Clearly, *The Birthday Party* omits the supernatural and the melodramatic without losing any intensity or mystery. The characters of the first play reappear modified: thus Rose = Meg; and Petey = Bert minus brutality; while the two men = Riley and the two men in *The Dumb Waiter*. But the enrichment of character is considerable when a blind Negro is turned into an Irishman and a Jew, the former brutal and silent, the latter full of worldly wisdom and good spirits. And there is a new character, Stanley Webber, of whose past we know so very little. Martin Esslin reasonably asks whether Goldberg and McCann are emissaries of some secret organization Stanley has betrayed (the I.R.A.?) or male nurses come belatedly from an asylum to fetch him back, or even, like the blind Negro, from another world?[31] They organize a party, brainwash Stanley (who insists it is not his birthday and tries to strangle Meg and rape Lulu), and carry him away. This action Esslin sees as an allegory of conformity wherein the artist is forced into respectability by emissaries from the bourgeois world: "It speaks plainly of the individual's pathetic search for security; of secret dreads and anxieties; of the terrorism of our world, so often embodied in false bonhomie and

bigoted brutality; of the tragedy that arises from lack of understanding between people on different levels of awareness."[32]
Bamber Gascoigne also sees the play in this light: "a neurotic
study of the pressure towards conformity brought to bear on a
second-rate young artist who has opted out of material success
and responsibility."[33] But Stanley is too decidedly second-rate,
if even that (we do not know whether his career is fact or fantasy); at best, he is an ambiguous representative of something,
and he is invited by Lulu to do for himself what is later done
for him.

Wellwarth interprets the play with more finality than any
other critic. He suggests that it is about the death of Stanley
Webber and specifically calls Goldberg and McCann "killers" (he
has the Hemingway story of that name in mind for some reason).
Where, however, does Goldberg talk about "his eminence as a
murderer with the same complacent pride that a bright young
executive might talk of his rise from an office boy's job"?[34] In
spite of this curious interpretation, Wellwarth thinks that *The
Birthday Party* is Pinter's best play, apparently because Artaud
would have approved of the end of Acts One and Two. To be
fair, a footnote specifically excludes imitation of Artaud; for, as
with allegory, such an imitation would suggest a plan, as an
allegory suggests an idea. And Pinter has always insisted on the
organic growth of his plays: "I think it is impossible—and certainly for me—to start writing a play from any kind of abstract
idea. . . . I start writing a play from an image of a situation and
a couple of characters involved, and these people always remain
for me quite real; if they were not, the play could not be written."
And: "Everything is funny; the great earnestness is funny; even
tragedy is funny. And I think what I try to do in my plays is to
get this recognizable reality of the absurdity of what we do and
how we behave and how we speak. The point about tragedy is
that it is *no longer funny.* It is funny and then it becomes no
longer funny."[35] Pinter has repeatedly stressed that he is dealing
not with an inability to communicate, but with a deliberate
evasion of communication: "Communication itself between people is so frightening that rather than do that there is continual
cross-talk, a continual talking about other things, rather than
what is at the root of their relationship."[36]

But Styan thinks that much of the vital comedy of the play has been sacrificed to the horrors of a subconscious hell:

Here in a squalid seaside boarding house a very proletarian Everyman called Stanley has buried himself from the world, without work, without hope and without washing himself. Unexpectedly a Jewish business man named Goldberg and an unfrocked Irish priest named McCann, agents of our imperious society, come to claim him. In the sinister scene of Stanley's so-called birthday party, in which a terrifying game of blindman's-buff is played with an obsessive intensity, Goldberg and McCann reduce their victim to speechlessness. Next day they dress him in "striped trousers, black jacket and white collar," and he is off in his bowler-hat, completely without identity.[37]

Such an interpretation makes of Stanley an Everyman, and ignoring the particular artist suggestions, it also makes large assumptions about the characters of the two men (the unfrocked priest could be another sick joke). If the plot line were simply this, there would be no reason for the emotions the play generates; or, to echo T. S. Eliot on *Hamlet*, we would be held by an emotion in *excess* of the facts as they appear.

Bernard Dukore, on the other hand, who sees Pinter's plays as one of the strangest types of theater to have emerged during the atomic age, describes them as a product of Maxim Gorki out of Charles Addams with Beckett as midwife and feels that the story line *is* only a convention. The plays of Pinter, for him, reflect the tensions and attitudes of a present-day England that is no longer a colonial power. They show man being reduced to a cipher of nonentity and his vain fight against that reduction. He is not so much unable as unwilling to communicate. Nor is it only conforming man that is being crushed into nonentity, but rebels too, of which the artist is naturally the chief. Thus *The Birthday Party* presents the extreme case: the artist, representing humanity, is reduced to conformity. In this sense, Dukore examines the two henchmen of society who bring pressure to bear, pointing out that they are symbolically right since they are representatives of the two traditional religions of Western civilization, Judaism and Catholicism (it would not be appropriate to send a Protestant to make Stanley conform!):

Each has several given names, and these carry connotations of tradition and religion. McCann is sometimes called Dermot (Diarmaid) and sometimes Seamus (James); Goldberg is called Nat (Nathan) but his wife used to call him Simey (Simon or Simeon), and his father called him Benjamin (Benny); and Goldberg has a son named Emmanuel whom he calls Timmy. Their names change according to the function they perform. For example, although Goldberg's father called him Benny (Benjamin was Jacob's youngest son and the favorite of his old age), he is in his present capacity called Nat, and just as Nathan the prophet, commanded directly by God, rebuked King David for having sinned against the Lord, and brought him back to the paths of righteousness, so does Nat, commanded directly by his organization, bring Stanley back to the paths of conformity. While Goldberg supplies the brains, McCann supplies the muscle (the Church Militant), and at one point exhorts a young lady to get down on her knees and confess. Thus a new Stanley is born.[38]

This interpretation takes the names of the characters very seriously. Such criticism needs the restraint of tact. If Pinter is using punning names, what of Boles and Webber? Webber at least could be *weaver* (of fantasy?); and, looking back at the first play, Hudd might be *guard* or *protection*. The process is erratic and inexhaustible, and such a close reading of names and allegorical meaning distracts from the impact of the play, which depends on what Wilson Knight, in his persuasive article on Kitchen Sink Drama, describes as numinous terrors.[39]

Discussing the vitality of contemporary drama, Knight points out that vitality comes from below, either what we call the subconscious mind (or "instinct") or from some lower social stratum; and in either case, this vitality can be called "Dionysian," favoring the unsophisticated and challenging orthodoxies. In contemporary drama, the kind of terror previously simply and conventionally (but also really) invoked with ghosts is now created by situations of difficulty, obscurity, or apprehension. Out of paradoxical states of mind, or objects or situations, out of what is irrational, the present-day dramatist produces an impact that must be called numinous—and Knight cites the possession of Stanley as he beats his drum at the end of Act One of *The Birthday Party*: "What we call the 'occult,' which means the 'hidden,' nowadays presses on us from tangible objects and paradoxical mental states; but it is no less frightening than the ghost-lore of earlier dramas." Thus, these effects today, Knight contends, will most probably come from material objects or human inventions and not from ghosts. It is the actual complication of life in a materialistic civilization that produces terror—a terror from which, presumably, Wilson Knight will not exclude the bureaucratic mysteries of Kafka.

This interpretaton explains the emotion without really explaining what causes the emotion. The need to be explicit where Pinter is not leads a critic like Ruby Cohn to see the two men as agents in a precise definition of our Judaeo-Christian heritage although why they should be faintly representing the I.R.A. as well is not clear. In fact, a precise social or political interpretation is undesirable, and probably J. T. Boulton is nearer the truth when he sees the play as a further exploitation of the need and nostalgia for the securities of childhood. The parody of mother-child relationship reaches a climax after the arrival of the sinister figures and the birthday present, when Stanley beats his drum savagely to frighten away the men who have come to destroy his security. The contrast between the vicious adult world and the safe night-lighted world of the child recalls the world of Graham Greene—seediness, professional thugs, traitors. The conversation Boulton finds psychologically true, since it catches the audience between what is true (verifiable fact) and true as dependent on the speaker's vision of his own significance.[40]

To verify partially is possible: the room is in a bad boarding house in a seaside town. It is not the tourist season, hence, the queerness of guests arriving and the fact that Stanley has been the only one. What Stanley's crime is we do not know—every conceivable accusation is thrown at him. McCann, as an Irishman, deals with politics and religion (treachery and heresy), and Goldberg, as a Jew and travelling salesman (hence the brief case), deals with sex and property: "Something for everyone, in fact: somewhere, the author seems to be telling his audience, you have done something—think hard and you may remember what it is—which will one day catch you out. The next time you answer a door to an innocent-looking stranger. . . ."[41] The ambiguity creates an atmosphere of uncertainty and doubt, but it also helps to generalize the fears and tensions to which particular, even peculiar, characters in Pinter's world are subject.

The problem is really whether or not the play succeeds in bringing together its many layers.

VI *Criticism of* The Birthday Party

At its first performance, the critics apparently thought that it had not brought together its many layers sufficiently well. But six years after the play was killed, *The Birthday Party* was revived, with Pinter himself as producer, in the Aldwych Theatre Summer Repertoire for 1964, where it received critical attention more respectful than that accorded it in 1958. There were, of course, critics who contrived to suggest that they had been and were still right. Philip Hope-Wallace in *The Guardian* (June 19) spoke of its revival "with all the dignity of a modern classic"; and he conceded that if Pinter neither explains nor apologizes, he nevertheless justifies himself: "Out of the remorseless alternations of banality and alusive (*sic*) menace—of word and look, out of the non sequiturs and incurious questionings, a mild but palpable theatrical excitement is distilled and hangs in the air like an indefinable odor of holiness." He recommended the play for addicts.

W. A. Darlington in the *Daily Telegraph* (June 19, 1964) was more honestly repentant, finding the play more enjoyable but still wanting to know what it was, exactly, that Stanley had done. For Bamber Gascoigne in *The Observer* (June 21, 1964), however, Pinter had made the situation all too plain, too ordinary. But Pinter's characters are not ordinary; they are a gallery of fascinating grotesques that the second cast failed to produce in the way the original cast had done. This emphasis on meaning was not really a gain, since the meaning remained (for Gascoigne) fairly ordinary: "the pressures and guilt brought to bear by ideas of family and success (Goldberg), politics and religion (McCann) on a second-rate artist who has opted out of society and wants just to vegetate." For Gascoigne, *The Birthday Party* was like *Waiting for Godot*, a fable that should lodge in the mind and breed implications. J. W. Lambert in *The Sunday Times* (June 21, 1964), who discussed the play at length, felt that its theatrical qualities were unmistakeable, as Pinter's "terrifying blend of pathos and hatred fuses unforgettably into the stuff of art."

The weeklies, because they have more time, could be expected to have more patience in creating a review. Jeremy Kingston in *Punch* (June 24, 1964) glossed the play in these terms: Act One —Stanley is being born (i.e., reluctantly pulled out of the room in which he has dwelt too long); Act Two—he is overwhelmed with statements of his guilt and past sins (i.e., perhaps the process of living); Act Three—we have the process of dying. But Kingston pointed out also that Pinter is a poet who always means more than two things at a time. He warned that although his dialogue is eminently quotable, this emphasized only the tape-recorder side of him: it is what goes on beneath that makes his work so exciting. David Pryce-Jones in *The Spectator* (June 26, 1964) produced what I assume was a parody—a conversation between Pryce and Jones with interlocutions by Pinter cribbed from the theater program. No doubt this review said something, but I found it so clever as to be incomprehensible.

Ronald Bryden, who wrote a more conventional review for *The New Statesman* (June 26, 1964), raised several points that are not new on the subject of drama and Pinter and life. Bryden began with the basic premise that the Pinter world "is a stage with nothing in the wings." All that is credible is what passes on the stage, and we are therefore dealing with the Theater of Situation, "the gospel according to Beckett and Pinter his prophet." This is good drama, but is it important or memorable? People are not like actors, and it would take more than a gallery of Pinter's special cases "to symbolize more than a partial or marginal truth about human character and motivation." But Pinter does not intend to symbolize—it is character that emerges, after all, from his plays, where even bogus character turns out to be stronger than situation. It is not, therefore, Pinter, Mr. Bryden concluded, that needs opposing, but something that he terms "Pinterism" and "Pinterites." Granted that such plays are popular because they are economical (three men in a bare room is easy to stage), there is the danger that we may find ourselves dominated by a "thin, inarticulate instant theater of situation." Pinter is "in a limited way, effective and entertaining," but his final importance may only be these qualities.

The initial premise of this argument (if, indeed, there is an argument here rather than a series of forays into cliché) is false. As in *The Caretaker*, there seems to be a triumph of theme over production. Thus, Petey works on the beach selling deck-chairs; there is general agreement on his occupation; there seems no reason to doubt either beach or deck-chairs, just as the cornflakes at breakfast must come from somewhere. In short, the action on the stage presupposes a world outside the stage and intercourse with it. When Bryden finally concluded that Pinter has a limited importance, the context seemed to imply a new cry for social reality. When he defined this thin and inarticulate (Pinter?) instant-theater of situation, Bryden wrote: "A theater which excludes character because character is not action; social reality, because social reality includes classes and culture references; history, because history had a large cast. . . ." Here he was surely asking for another type of play and expressing a preference for it, a play presumably by Brecht or Wesker. But then, Pinter is not Brecht, just as he is not Beckett.

It is absurd to have to stress that Pinter writes Pinter plays and that they are just as much about life as, say, Wesker's plays are about life, in spite of all Wesker's pretensions at social realism, history, and class structure. The so-called working class in Wesker's trilogy, located in East End London, bears no resemblance to the working class of the 1930's in the West Riding of Yorkshire (nor, for that matter, is the R.A.F. in *Chips with Everything* remarkably convincing, as a comparison with Henry Livings's *Nil Carborundum* [1962] shows). Pinter's limitations, if that is the right word, are simply any dramatist's limitations in having to put life on a stage for two hours and say something important. If the danger of Pinterism is that it tries to turn an image into a world view and tries to deny the validity of logic and language and the notion of the continuity of personality, there is every reason for denying these validities. Brecht's *Mother Courage and Her Children* offers no better treatment of the basic problems.

In fact, this second production of *The Birthday Party*, holding off the horror aspects and allowing itself to be taken as broad comedy (noticeably changed as the production got into its stride) left little for the critic to say, as John Russell Taylor rather whimsically suggests in his review in the August issue of *Plays and Players*; in this less than ideal reading, *The Birthday Party* "is something unique in the contemporary Theater" and should not be missed.

This production had a rightness about it the sense of which developed with re-seeing. I was prepared to agree with Bamber Gascoigne's description and disagreement until, in retrospect, and after seeing the play again, the explanation struck me even more forcibly: because the explanation was clearer, the menace was all the more unreasonable. Pinter also delicately threw emphasis upon certain aspects that the text cannot. Stanley was stronger as a character, bandying words with the strangers, torturing Meg with the haunting idea of her being carted away in a wheelbarrow, a fear she still retains at the end of the play. The extremely slow action of the play justifies itself gradually. Thus, McCann's irritatingly slow tearing up of a newspaper in Act Two was matched significantly by a rapid tearing up of the newspaper in Act Three. The broad comedy of the opening darkens only slowly, and if we did not feel much sympathy for anyone in particular by the end of the play, we were frightened into recognizing that what had just been seen was something more than an allegory about an artist in society, something we might conceivably apply, if we dared, to ourselves, whatever our class, cultural references, or history might be. This feeling matures later in *The Caretaker* into the recognition that we all have our Sidcups; and, if those Sidcups are not cosmic, they are none the less frightening nor ultimately without eschatalogical implications.

VII   The Dumb Waiter

The Dumb Waiter, not produced until 1960, was first presented at the Hampstead Theatre Club and later at the Royal Court Theatre. It was written in 1957, along with *The Room* and *The Birthday Party*. It takes as its subject the two agents in the latter play, but it shows the predicament of the victimizers not the victim: "In *The Birthday Party* the hired killers (if they are hired killers) appear as all-powerful and inscrutable: where Stanley is menaced, they are menace personified, invulnerable beings, one might suppose, from another world, emissaries of death. But no, *The Dumb Waiter* assures us, hired killers are just men like anyone else; they can only obey orders, and while menacing others they themselves can be menaced."[42] Sinko expresses the theme another way: "When the functionary begins to reflect on the meaning of his job, he must die. The mechanism is a self-regulating one, hence the appropriateness of the ambiguous meaning of the Polish title: Samoobsluga, Self-service. Whatever one might think, the job has to go on. Just as in *The Birthday Party* we have not come close to the secret Court or the Authority living in the castle or at the top of the lift: we have just seen it work from another side."[43] This is a more accurate, if less precise, description than Taylor's summary; except in conjunction with *The Dumb Waiter*, there is no reason to assume that Goldberg and McCann *are* killers. Indeed, "Monty," in connection with the promised yacht, may well be another seaside resort rather than a psychiatrist or secret court. But, more significantly, McCann is asking questions, and even the assured Goldberg loses confidence and has to break a chest-expander to prove his fitness. The menacers are uneasy in *The Birthday Party*, and it is this unease that is explored in *The Dumb Waiter*, a genuine comedy of menace set in a basement flat in Birmingham. And in this play Pinter begins to use silence as part of his dialogue.

In his article "Between the Lines" written for *The Sunday Times*, Pinter speaks of the two silences—one when no word is spoken, and the second when a torrent of words is used as part of the continual evasion of communication. If the mystification in *The Dumb Waiter* is both more subtle and witty than in *The Birthday Party*, it is frequently because Pinter has learned how to play off a silent character with a loquacious one and also how to use total silence to emphasize edginess and the failure or unwillingness to communicate. Gus cannot bear silence, and Ben resents conversation; in each case, the method produces thought and communication.

The basement room of this play has no windows, but it has two doors, one opening into the unknown, the other, into a defective lavatory. In this room two men of no particular age, called Ben and Gus, are waiting. Ben is reading a newspaper from which he occasionally reads diverting passages and from behind which he watches irritably as Gus moves restlessly about the room or makes frequent visits to the defective toilet. Their rambling conversation is about trivial matters—items in the newspaper, the crockery they have been provided with, who is playing whom at football next Saturday—trivia interspersed with questions from Gus about the length of the job they are on and what time "he" is likely to get in touch with them. This more serious probing is resented by Ben as excessively, it seems, as is Gus's annoyance with the room: Gus likes to have "a bit of a view." Ben, with his woodwork and model boats, replies that Gus ought to have a hobby. But Gus goes on asking questions. Why, for example, did Ben stop the car early that morning when he thought Gus was asleep? These odd remarks, running through an average conversation on football and ordinary life, combined with the tension that obviously exists between Ben and Gus, gradually build up a sense of something sinister behind the casual presence of two men waiting to do a job in a Birmingham basement flat.

When an envelope containing 12 matches is pushed under the door and a revolver is snatched from under a pillow, we become more and more certain that these men are not ordinary workers, that the job is no everyday one, that, in fact, they are two hired assassins, part of a large and mysterious organization, and that their occupation is travelling up and down the country killing people to order. Thus, the seemingly trivial argument over the phrase "light a kettle" is more than a semantic quibble. It summarizes the relative positions of the two men. When Ben wearily forgets and says "Put on the bloody kettle," the inadequacy of his position of not questioning is revealed. Such arguments are a comic but tactful foundation for the main question of the play. Moreover, Gus's irritation over smelly sheets, crockery that is not so good as it has been, the lack of tea, not having a window, and being permanently on call is really irritation with the job itself, a reflection of the qualms he has begun to feel about it:

GUS: I was just thinking about that girl, that's all. (GUS *sits on his bed.*) She wasn't much to look at, I know, but still. It was a mess though, wasn't it? What a mess. Honest, I can't remember a mess like that one. They don't seem to hold together like men, women. A looser texture, like. Didn't she spread, eh? She didn't half spread. Kaw! But I've been meaning to ask you. (BEN *sits up and clenches his eyes.*) Who clears up after we've gone? I'm curious about that. Who does the clearing up? Maybe they don't clear up. Maybe they just leave them there, eh? What do you think? How many jobs have we done? Blimey, I can't count them. What if they never clear anything up after we've gone.

BEN (*pityingly*): You mutt. Do you think we're the only branch of this organization? Have a bit of common. They got departments for everything.

[65]

Gus: What, cleaners and all?
Ben: You birk!
Gus: No, it was that girl made me start to think . . . .[44]

Thought, however, is prevented by a clatter from the back of the room, where there is a serving hatch or dumb waiter that suddenly starts to descend noisily with orders on it for food. The two gunmen, anxious not to be discovered, try to fulfill those orders with what food they have with them, an Eccles cake, a bar of chocolate, half a pint of milk, and a packet of potato chips. When Ben accuses Gus of hiding the one Eccles cake from him, it is, in view of the end of the play, rather an ironic reproach. But we are made to sense throughout the play, particularly if that morning wait in the car was a crisis of conscience on Ben's part, that a great deal of Ben's edginess stems from knowing or suspecting what he has to do and from faintly resenting it. The knowledge that Ben has to get rid of his mate could very well account for his excessive resentment at the start of the play.

The orders for food continue to arrive, becoming more and more exotic, from macaroni pastitsio and ormitha macarounda to scampi. The two men shout up the serving hatch that they have sent up everything. Since this has no effect, they decide to send a written message. At this point, they notice a speaking tube that will only work for Ben, who speaks into it with great deference and is told something. Ben and Gus then rehearse the murder in a duologue in canonic manner that, significantly, leaves out the instruction of when Gus is to take his gun out. After this, the two gunmen return to the newspaper game, but this time on a more muted level. While Gus is once more in the defective lavatory, Ben gets his orders—to shoot the next person to come in through the outside door. When Gus enters through that door, Ben faces him gun in hand and, presumably, shoots him at the end of the slow curtain.

The main element of comedy is provided by the dialogue—conversation to pass the time while Gus and Ben wait, not for Godot, but for orders. Their moral indignation roused over items in the newspaper (about a man of 87 who crawled under a lorry and was run over or the child of eight who killed a cat) culminates in the plain assumption that they are just doing a job, even if that job is the unusual one of committing murder; and, as long as they regard it as that, they are adequate gunmen. The discussions on football, making tea, and what to do on Saturday are, or grow, terrifying as we see not merely what the men are, but that Gus is no longer a good gunman (he has begun to think about the victims and ask questions about the organization). We begin to suspect that the orders from above—from the landlord of this house—will lead to tragedy. Clearly, this play satisfies the postulate of Ionesco that tragedy should always be fused with hilarious farce. The play is much more comic than either of the preceding plays. There is a victim, presumably, but the play is *about* the difference between Ben (the dumb waiter) and Gus (who by his questioning is rebelling). Whereas Ben accepts orders and is an almost perfect cog in a larger machine, Gus is becoming an individual and must be eliminated. Ironically, this very elimination might in turn unsettle Ben (a feasible interpretation from the text, although I have seen no production that positively incorporates it), who might then have to be eliminated.

VIII   Critical Interpretations

Both Dukore and Cohn accept Gus's death by an organization that resents the probing; Styan feels that the play ends abruptly with the death of Gus; but Taylor rightly reminds us that the end is a slow curtain with no shooting. However we interpret the end, which is itself clear, whatever interpretation we put on it, Pinter succeeds in making the mysterious upstairs element, so melodramatic and sentimental in *The Room*, into an additional element of comedy in *The Dumb Waiter*. As Esslin points out, there is a great deal of fun in the sight of heaven bombarding two solemn gunmen with demands for exotic food. Perhaps this abundant comic element makes the play seem slighter, less symbolic than its equivalent one-act play, *The Room*. Boulton feels that *The Dumb Waiter* lacks stature, having the air of a dramatized anecdote. But it is a very funny play in which the air of menace is beautifully sustained. Boulton, to my mind, underestimates the skill with which the dialogue produces two stories. J. W. Lambert's introduction to the play in the Penguin edition sums up the worth of the play admirably:

The Dumb Waiter, for instance, has no perceptible intellectual content at all. Its drama, like all Mr. Pinter's, is not only less intellectual but more interior than Mr. Arden's, let alone Mr. Hall's. This glimpse of two hired killers is told not merely without heightened prose but in the lowest common denominator of human speech–a dialogue in which every phrase is drawn almost straight from life at a level of intellectual vacancy which might seem the death of drama; but which is handled with such a sure command of pause and repetition that it evokes simultaneously the laughter of contemptuous recognition and a shiver of dread. As within ourselves, on the one hand open abysses of bottomless inanity, on the other loom the fearful crags of an irrational, implacable cruelty.

Bizarre and claustrophobic as it is, Mr. Pinter's exploration of the lower depths has an unmistakeable, if indefinable relevance to life as we live it. But it is not, of course, explicitly sociological.[45]

IX A Slight Ache *and Other Plays*

Besides these three stage plays, Pinter's early work includes plays for radio and revue sketches: *A Slight Ache* (1959); sketches for two revues in the same year; and the two radio plays in 1960, *A Night Out* and *The Dwarfs*. Some of these have since been televised or staged. In this group of sketches and plays Pinter modified the techniques and themes of the first three plays of 1957. In particular, he altered the tone of the themes.

A Slight Ache, originally written for radio, is a play for which Pinter has great affection. Written in the post-*Birthday Party* failure period, it established, for him, the right to write as he pleased. Its setting, if characteristic, is different: an elegant country house with a garden in which Edward and Flora live. If breakfast between Edward and Flora, with which the play opens, reminds us of *The Room* or of *The Birthday Party*, the social status of the two characters is obviously different, and the room is extended to include the garden, the subject of the argument opening the play. This argument is crystallized for us and for the characters by the arrival of a wasp, which Edward kills with great satisfaction by trapping it in the marmalade pot and then by pouring boiling water on it.

Once the wasp is despatched, Edward suddenly reveals his worry about a matchseller who has been standing at the back gate for two months. Both Edward and Flora use the word "bullock" to describe him. In some way, he is a catalyst for the inadequacy of the relationship between Edward and Flora. Thus, when Flora calls her husband "Beddie Weddie," Edward's annoyance is surely only partly because she is treating him as a baby. Finally, Edward insists that Flora invite the matchseller in; and the gross, revolting, but completely silent old man becomes the focus of the histories of both characters. From these histories, which may or may not be true, the play builds up the antagonisms between Edward and Flora—the inadequacy of Edward and the desires of Flora (her Laurentian rape speech is so wittily told it might be fantasy).

The character of Edward begins to emerge as the more significant; he is asking questions. To ask questions in Pinter is always dangerous, as we have seen in *The Dumb Waiter*. The act of questioning appearances, motives, or consequences invites catastrophe. For Flora, the problem of who or what the matchseller is is soon settled—she gives the matchseller a name, Barnabas (son of exhortation, i.e., by encouragement); and, in naming him, she solves the problem of his identity. Barnabas becomes for her the desirable and submissive combination of child, husband, and lover that the apparently dominant Edward never could be. Edward, however, begins to show what is behind the bullying, self-contained façade of the early breakfast scene. Since the play principally rests on him, Pinter gives him two long speeches to Flora's one. His first speech is a history, as is Flora's; but the second one is less a history and more a probe in which he tries to define the matchseller, put a name on him, and put him into a context which is comprehensible. He uses such questions and statements as: what game do you play? or, you remind me of Cavendish. This lack of definition contrasts sharply with yesterday's clarity of vision:

Yesterday now, it was clear, clearly defined, so clearly.
(*Pause.*)
The garden, too, was sharp, lucid, in the rain, in the sun.
(*Pause.*)
My den, too, was sharp, arranged for my purpose . . . quite
    satisfactory.
(*Pause.*)

The house, too, was polished, all the banisters were polished, and the
stair rods, and the curtain rods.
(*Pause.*)
My desk was polished, and my cabinet.
(*Pause.*)
I was polished. (*Nostalgic.*) . . . .[46]

Now all this brightness and clarity merely dazzles Edward
into blindness. At this point the opening argument over the
names of flowers becomes more understandable. So does the significance of Flora's last entrance, when she offers Barnabas an
orderly polished house: her husband has been reduced to the
silence of the matchseller (just as Rose became blind, and
Stanley dumb). Edward is asking questions and expects to be
given information by questions asked by Barnabas. But, when
Barnabas says nothing, Edward is obliged to invent questions for
him. Before this silence, his crisp English middle-class reticence
breaks down into an orgy of confession and self-examination that
from the beginning is concerned with the basic question: who or
what is the matchseller? Desperately, Edward tries to pin him
down: for over two months he has looked at the matchseller in
all weathers from all angles and in all lights. The present examination breaks down the examiner; and, like Len (*The Dwarfs*)
and Aston (*The Caretaker*), the wish to know more clearly and
to answer the great question—Who are you?—ends the play with
the substitution of Edward for the matchseller.

Basically, there are the usual properties in *A Slight Ache*: a
room, uneasy inhabitants, and the threat of intrusion that will
destroy a precarious if unhappy cosiness. But the threat is more
completely located inside the characters themselves than before
(we could compare the silent matchseller with Ionesco's Killer);
indeed, the audience could not verify on the radio whether the
matchseller really existed outside the imagination of Edward and
Flora. John Russell Brown sees this play as Pinter's simplest:

An intruding wasp and a stationary, mysterious matchseller set off
the interplay between husband and wife, Edward and Flora. This is
ordinary bickering, Flora taking the punishment. But when the matchseller is brought into the house and remains silent, each character
becomes more uneasy. Their rivalry is deep enough to force them to
overcome fears, and each contrives to speak with the matchseller

alone. Then, irritated and challenged by his continual silence, they express their thoughts compulsively and powerfully; their habitual reserve is broken and they utter their hidden irrational fears and demands, as if by possession. Flora treats the stranger as a lover and as a husband to be cossetted, while Edward tries to justify himself in the stranger's eyes by bragging of his own physical achievement, and in this earlier phrases are repeated, now "respoken" or revealing their true motivation. The play ends when Flora re-enters, talking with ease to the silent man, and takes him off to lunch; she pauses only to give Edward the tray of matches to hold. Here the expression of hidden resources of character at the end gives the play a brief development in the usual sense of the word.[47]

This last sentence, even in context, is more enigmatic than the play. Here the room has a window and a view (anticipating *The Lover* in setting and theme), and the menace is invited in (as in *The Caretaker*) to play a completely passive role—to become, in fact, no more than the object in relation to which Edward and Flora act out their inadequacies. But whereas Flora gathers strength until she can exchange men, Edward breaks down when confronted with the silent matchseller. This subject is explored in a short story written about 1953 called "The Examination" and is still further developed in another short story, "Tea Party."[48]

X "The Examination"

"The Examination," first published in the 1959 summer issue of *Prospect* and reprinted with *The Collection* and *The Lover* in 1963, does not seem to be simply an academic examination in spite of the presence of chalk and a blackboard. It could be compared with the interview sketch "Applicant," although it is written in orotund, quasi-philosophical prose. Perhaps less a short story than a sketch-monologue, it does, as Taylor suggests, provide a note to *A Slight Ache*. The story contains three favorite Pinter motifs: domination, a room, and silence. In the examination of Kullus by the Examiner (the "I" of the story), we trace the gradual change of the dominant to the dominated, thus anticipating the theme of *The Servant*. This switch is conducted mainly in silence and in a move from the initial condition:

Frequently his [Kullus'] disposition would be such that little could be achieved by insistence, or by persuasion. When Kullus was disposed to silence I invariably acquiesced, and prided myself on those occasions with tactical acumen. But I did not regard these silences as intervals, for they were not, and neither, I think, did Kullus so regard them. For if Kullus fell silent, he did not cease to participate in our examination. Never, at any time, had I reason to doubt his active participation, through word and through silence, between interval and interval, and I recognised what I took to be his devotion as actual and unequivocal, besides, as it seemed to me, obligatory. And so the nature of our silence within the frame of our examination, and the nature of our silence outside the frame of our examination, were entirely opposed.

Finally, ". . . the time came when Kullus initiated intervals at his own inclination, and pursued his courses at will, and I was able to remark some consistency in his behavior. For now I followed him in his courses without difficulty, and there was no special duration for interval or examination, but one duration, in which I participated. My devotion was actual and unequivocal. I extended my voluntary co-operation, and made no objection to procedure."[49]

The transference takes place in a room belonging to "I," but previous action has been in Kullus' room. The window is open, the curtains are open, and Kullus is pulled into the light. The properties of this room are emphasized to stamp it as the Examiner's room; thus, there is no fire in the grate as in Kullus' room. At first, Kullus does not acknowledge the differences, but by the end, he has not merely noticed the differences but has begun to remove them:

And when he removed the blackboard, I offered no criticism. And when he closed the curtains I did not object.

For we were now in Kullus's room.

Finally, there is the problem of silence, one clearly crucial as the stimulus of transference. We follow the Examiner's inability to understand this and his increasing anxiety in trying to define it, which finally leads him to accept his own Examination by Kullus:

And so gradually, where this occurred, I began to take the only course open to me, and terminated the intervals arbitrarily, cutting short the proposed duration, when I could no longer follow him, and was no longer dominant.

By the end, he has changed places with Kullus.

[72]

The language here is reminiscent in its philosophical content of the language of *The Dwarfs*. It must be remembered that both *A Slight Ache* and *The Dwarfs* were plays for radio, a medium giving wider scope than the stage for Pinter the poet, the user of words. They are essentially plays to be listened to. *A Slight Ache* also marks the end of Pinter's first period, one of relative obscurity. *A Slight Ache* was commissioned for the British Broadcasting Corporation "Third Program," which serves only a minority audience; *The Dumb Waiter* had been produced first in Germany; and neither *The Room* nor *The Birthday Party* had been exactly successful with either the critics or the audiences. Henceforth, Pinter's public impact was greater, and the description, "comedy of menace," also becomes less and less apt.

XI   *Revue Sketches*

It is possible that writing revue sketches helped Pinter to develop pure comedy, although even these sketches are not that, tinged as they are with the sad, the pathetic, and the sinister. Pinter has refused to publish two of them—"Special Offer" and "Getting Acquainted"; indeed, the latter is, according to him, lost. The former, however, is a brief, eminently quotable account of a B.B.C. lady disturbed by the offer of men for sale in a leading London store. Mr. Pinter has kindly allowed the sketch to be printed here:

SECRETARY (*at desk in office*): Yes, I was in the rest room at Swan and Edgars, having a little rest. Just sitting there, interfering with nobody, when this old crone suddenly came right up to me and sat beside me. You're on the staff of the B.B.C. she said, aren't you? As a matter of fact I am, I said. What can I do for you? I've got just the thing for you, she said, and put a little card into my hand. Do you know what was written on it? MEN FOR SALE! What on earth do you mean? I said. Men, she said, all sorts shapes and sizes, for sale. What on earth can you *possibly mean?* I said. It's an international congress, she said, got up for the entertainment and relief of lady members of the civil service. You can hear some of the boys we've got speak through a microphone, especially for your pleasure, singing little folk tunes we're sure you've never heard before. Tea is on the house and every day we have the very best pastries. For the cabaret at teatime the boys do a rare dance imported all the way from Buenos Aires, dressed in nothing but a pair of cricket pads. Every

single one of them is tried and tested, very best quality, and at very reasonable rates. If you like one of them by any of his individual characteristics you can buy him, but for you not at retail price. As you work for the B.B.C. we'll be glad to make a special reduction. If you're at all dissatisfied you can send him back within seven days and have your money refunded. That's *very* kind of you, I said, but as a matter of fact I've just been on leave, I start work tomorrow and am perfectly refreshed. And I left her where she was. Men for Sale! What an extraordinary idea! I've never heard of anything so outrageous, have you? Look—here's the card.
(*Pause.*)
Do you think it's a joke . . . or serious?

This sketch strikes me as extremely rich in suggestiveness. But beneath the absurdity, the logical premise is: if there are callgirls, why not callboys for tired women executives?

Two of the sketches in print are interview scenes, "Trouble in the Works" and "Applicant." The first is a skit on technological terminology in heavy engineering that is reminiscent of the do-it-yourself fantasy in *The Caretaker*. A works manager receives complaints from the workers' representative about certain objects they are making and to which they have taken a dislike:

WILLS: They've just taken a turn against the whole lot of them, I tell you. Male elbow adaptors, tubing nuts, grub screws, internal fan washers, dog points, half dog points, white metal bushes—
FIBBS: But not, surely, my lovely parallel male stud couplings.
WILLS: They hate and detest your lovely parallel male stud couplings, and the straight flange pump connectors, and back nuts, and front nuts, *and* the bronzedraw off cock with handwheel and the bronzedraw off cock without handwheel![50]

And when Fibbs, the manager, asks despairingly what the men do want to make, the answer is brisk and pointed: Brandy Balls.

In the second interview sketch, an applicant for a job is fitted with electrodes and bombarded with impossible questions until he suffers a complete collapse, a situation half way between the interrogations of *The Birthday Party* and the shock treatment in *The Caretaker*, but one lacking the seriousness of either. The other three sketches show two or more characters put into relation to one another and allowed to interact: "The Black and White" (two old tramp women compare notes on how to pass the night); "Last to Go" (a newspaper seller and the proprietor of a coffee stall discuss which paper is last to be sold);[51] and "Request Stop" (a slightly mad woman pesters a man at a bus stop with a question and then loudly maintains he has made an improper suggestion to her). All of these sketches are, in a sense, about the failure or unwillingness to communicate.

XII   A Night Out

Pinter also produced two more radio plays, *A Night Out* and *The Dwarfs*, the first of which was almost immediately transferred to television, where it had a record audience of between 15 and 18 million viewers. Like the plays that followed it, *A Night Out* shows the shift to comedy achieved by Pinter in his work on the revue sketches. These sketches he regards as important as his plays: "As far as I am concerned there is no real difference between my sketches and my plays. In both I am interested primarily in people: I want to present living people to the audience, worthy of their interest primarily because they *are*, they exist, not because of any moral the author may draw from them."[52]

It is tempting to regard this shift to more completely comic plays as progress from nonrealism to a greater realism, but, in fact, the menacers in *The Birthday Party* belong to the normal world and behave more like ordinary people than not, while the gunmen in *The Dumb Waiter* are shown as ordinary people doing a job (admittedly an extraordinary job by most standards), and in both plays violence has been eliminated. If we exclude what was done to the wasp, violence and menace are almost totally passive in *A Slight Ache*, anticipating their exclusion from *The Caretaker*, in which fear is a practical joke and a clash of personalities leads finally to displacement. *A Night Out* also shows the new directness and simplicity reflected in the television play, *Night School* (see Chapter 4), and *The Caretaker* (see Chapter 3). Its title, *A Night Out*, suggests a breaking out of the room and sounds a note of defiance. But, as Laurence Kitchin briskly remarks, "room service is quickly resumed when the hero picks up a genteel tart."[53]

The play opens with Albert Stokes trying to escape from a possessive mother who will not admit that her husband is dead or that grandma has been dead for ten years—will not admit these facts linguistically at any rate—and whose principal worry is that Albert will grow up and leave her, a worry focused on the idea that he will get a girl friend:

MOTHER (*following*): Albert.
ALBERT: What?
MOTHER: I want to ask you a question.
ALBERT: What?
MOTHER: Are you leading a clean life?
ALBERT: A clean life?
MOTHER: You're not leading an unclean life, are you?
ALBERT: What are you talking about?
MOTHER: You're not messing about with girls, are you? You're not going to go messing about with girls tonight?
ALBERT: Don't be so ridiculous.
MOTHER: Answer me, Albert. I'm your mother.
ALBERT: I don't know any girls.
MOTHER: If you're going to the firm's party, there'll be girls there, won't there? Girls from the office?
ALBERT: I don't like them, any of them.
MOTHER: You promise?
ALBERT: Promise what?
MOTHER: That . . . that you won't upset your father.
ALBERT: My father? How can I upset my father? You're always talking about upsetting people who are dead!
MOTHER: Oh, Albert, you don't know how you hurt me, you don't know the hurtful way you've got, speaking of your poor father like that.
ALBERT: But he is dead.
MOTHER: He's not. He's living! (*Touching her breast.*) In here! And this is his house![54]

The scene shifts to a coffee stall where two of Albert's friends from the office, Seeley and Kedge (the former played by Pinter himself), are discussing Albert's recent depression, which is spoiling his game of football. At this point, Pinter shifts to a short scene that shows Albert finally escaping. He comes to the coffee stall, where his friends tease him about a girl (who, they say, is attracted to Albert), his poor game of football, and his mother. The final shot of Act One on television shows the mother laying out a game of patience and the clock ticking on the mantelpiece.

The second act is the firm's party to say good-by to an old and trusted member of the company, Mr. Ryan. Here another friend of Albert's asks his girl friend's friend, Eileen, to pretend to be friendly with Albert for a joke. Eileen agrees to do so. During the formal speech of farewell, however, Eileen lets out a scream and claims that she has been interfered with, and Albert is blamed. When the firm's accountant Gidney taunts him with being a mother's boy, Albert, after hitting him, leaves the party. In the television production, it was possible to make it quite clear that the gentleman who pinched Eileen was Mr. Ryan. On the radio, this precise identification was, of course, impossible. The second scene shows Albert's mother asleep in a disorder of playing cards, the clock at 12, and Albert creeping in. She immediately awakens and, seeing his disheveled appearance, assumes he has been messing about with girls. She launches into a long speech on his wickedness in which leaving her to go and mess about with girls is confused with his leaving dinner uneaten. Albert breaks down, and the scene closes as he raises the clock above her head as if he were going to hit her with it.

Act Three shows Albert back at the coffee stall, which is now closed, where he meets a tart who takes him back to her flat. There she tries to give him the impression that she is really a refined lady with a daughter attending a select boarding school at Hereford. She complains when Albert swears and insists that she take off his shoes, use the ash tray, and show other marks of domesticity. Albert pretends to be an assistant director in films, and this pretense stimulates the girl to reveal her own longing for the sexual, violent, glamorous life she thinks he must lead as a film director. Albert, who ignores her rambling monologue, suddenly picks up the clock. Alarmed, the girl begins to psychoanalyze him; but he deliberately stubs a cigarette out on the carpet, threatens her with the clock, breaks the photograph of the daughter, exposing it as a lie, and, having made her put his shoes on him, leaves, casually flipping her half a crown. The final scene shows his return to his mother, who welcomes him back as if nothing had happened:

Listen, Albert, I'll tell you what I'm going to do. I'm going to forget it. You see? I'm going to forget all about it. We'll have your holiday in a fortnight. We can go away. *She strokes his hand.* It's not as if

you're a bad boy . . . you're a good boy . . . I know you are . . . it's
not as if you're really bad, Albert, you're not . . . you're not bad,
you're good . . . you're not a bad boy, Albert, I know you're not. . . .
(*Pause.*)
You're good, you're not bad, you're a good boy . . . I know you are
. . . you are, aren't you?[55]

Unfortunately for Albert, she is right: the night out is over.

There is no mystery in the play; the dreams of both the tart
and Albert we know to be only dreams, the photograph is identified by the inscription on the back, and even the person who
interfered with Eileen is identified in the directions for the television production. The play is, first, about the need to communicate between a mother and a son and, second, about the need
for lonely people to have illusions, the *need* to lie. Basically, it
concerns Albert and his mother, the Stanley-Meg situation. However, since Albert has not chosen the situation, he resents it; nor
is he able, as Stanley does, to turn his mother's stupidity to his
own advantage. He feels guilty going to the party. The party,
then, is bound to be disastrous because he has gone against his
mother's wishes. And, even when he resorts to violence, he has
to be content with what Taylor calls "a substitute victory" against
a substitute victim; for example, he reproaches the girl, as he
does his mother, for endless talking. His mother's willingness to
forget and her remaining unharmed show that nothing Albert
can now do really matters.

XIII   The Dwarfs

Finally, in 1960, the B.B.C. "Third Program" broadcast Pinter's
last radio play to date, *The Dwarfs*, which followed the stage
success of *The Caretaker* and which Pinter himself produced on
the stage of the New Arts Theatre in September, 1963. Of this
play, Taylor concedes that it is the most difficult and the most
daunting to popular taste.[56] And Wellwarth concludes that it is
impossible to make anything definite of it.[57] The reactions of
critics and audiences in 1963, in spite of a magnificently sensitive
performance by John Hurt in the main part, continue to justify
the judgment of both Taylor and Wellwarth. The play was written for radio, a medium Pinter finds naturally attractive because

it allows him more freedom to experiment than any other medium—to experiment with both form and content. Thus, *The Dwarfs* was an extremely valuable play for Pinter, although he admits that it may have been incomprehensible to the audience.[58]

The Dwarfs is based on an unpublished novel written in 1953–1957 that has four characters—three men and a girl. In the play, there are only three men, Len, Pete, and Mark. The novel was, apparently, partly autobiographical (one of the characters in the play still shares Pinter's Portuguese ancestry with him). Written over too long a period, the novel contained too many styles, and only the things Pinter felt worth exploring were used in his radio play.[59]

XIV *The Action of the Play*

The Dwarfs opens with two typical Pinter characters, Pete and Len, who are waiting in Mark's flat for his return. Initially, Pete and Len remind us of the two gunmen in *The Dumb Waiter* because of their desultory conversation, mainly about food and Mark, and particularly because of Len's incessant questions and Pete's irritation at them. We learn nothing about Pete, but we do gather that Len has a casual job as a porter at Euston station and prefers night work. The excitable nature of Len's interest in things justifies Pete's early comment: "You'll be ready for the looney bin next week if you go on like this." Pete, in contrast to Len, is thoroughly noncommittal; even when Len examines his palm and pronounces Pete a homicidal maniac, he remains unperturbed.

The arrival of Mark ends this scene. The next takes place in Len's room. The text makes no note of this, but the production showed that Len's room was old, inherited from the family, and rather like an Edgar Allan Poe room in decor and furnishing. Here Len tries to establish his fixture by defining, in a manner reminiscent of Ionesco's language-primer dialogue, his table, his chair, his bowl of fruit, and so on.[60] Against this fixture, which makes all "clear and abundant" but which is also a "manacle," runs the idea that the room moves ("to a dead halt," ironically!). At the moment all is ordered, in its place; and Len is wedged: "There are no voices. They make a hole in my side." Since *The Dwarfs* is a play for voices and since we can treat it as poetic, the hole-in-the-side image could have a religious significance—it is repeated later—but it does not make Len a Christ figure. It reminds us of certain connections, just as Wellwarth may be right in seeing Mark as a papal symbol.[61] This soliloquy is interrupted by the arrival of Mark in a new suit that is described, or defined, in a music hall patter played out between Len and Mark. Once more the conversation is inconsequential, but behind it is the desire to put a label or a price on everything—a desire that holds together statements like: "There is a time and place for everything" and "The price of butter is going up."[62]

Mark's presence in the room, although he never mentions the room, is a challenge: Len insists that he wants no curiosity there. Since curiosity is a mark of a Pinter victim and is liberally displayed by Len and rarely, if ever, by Mark, this remark can be taken as ironic and as self-commentary. It leads to Len's second statement about the room. In his first description, while conceding mobility (the room rearranges itself if one stops watching it), he emphasizes "fixture"—albeit an imprisoning one. Len now emphasizes "mobility" or change. One cannot, he asserts, rely on the natural behavior of a room, however much one wants to. He uses the analogy of sitting in a railway compartment to show unknowability. From his window he can see lights moving that he knows are still and move only because he moves; or rather, because he is still but being moved. Only when moving can he know objects, yet objects in stillness alone can be known. This is a complicated way of saying that what we think we know can be false, and in the following scene, Pete suggests putting the troublesome furniture in a boat and parking it (not moving it). Pete delivers a lecture to Len summed up in the line: "Giving up the ghost isn't so much a failure as a tactical error."

Pete insists that Len pull himself together, or he will be locked up. When Len protests that things change every minute, Pete replies that he should discriminate: "You've got no idea how to preserve a distance between what you smell and what you think about it. You haven't got the faculty for making a simple distinction between one thing and another. Every time you walk out of this door you go straight over a cliff. What you've got to do is nourish the power of assessment. How can you hope to assess and verify anything if you walk about with your nose stuck between your feet all day long?"[63]

Pete then warns Len that Mark is no good for him and follows

Comedies of Menace

this with a surrealistic account of a dream: of himself in a subway station in which everybody's face was peeling off, rotting and blistering—which reduces Len to groans. It is possible that Pete's nightmare, deliberately thrust on the unstable Len, acts like Goldberg's speeches on Stanley. If, in fact, Pete and Mark are another form of menacers, there is an ironic extension of their powers in the dwarfs themselves. Who or what the dwarfs are, we are not told; they simply organize, carry out a job of some sort, and leave (like fantastic Goldbergs and McCanns?). They are skilled laborers, and their trade is not without risk. Thus, they do seem to be a phantasmal representation of the organization that hires Ben and Gus or Goldberg and McCann. We do know that in some way Len's standing with them depends on Pete and Mark.

In the next scene, Len, possibly influenced by Pete's dream, asks Mark about his face, and Mark warns Len that Pete is no good for him. Len interrupts this to state once more the intimate involvement of Len, Pete, Mark, and the dwarfs, using the conjugation of a verb: "he sits, I sit; they stand, I squat." As the dialogue becomes more and more interior, the play seems to consist of a steady progression into Len's private world. Often, scenes with Pete and Mark seem more presented by Len than directly experienced by us. The dwarfs, according to Len, have gone off on a picnic, leaving him to clean up their garbage. In a soliloquy, he visualizes his two friends as seagull and spider:

Pete walks by the—gull. Slicing gull. Gull. Down. He stops. Stone. Watches. Rat corpse in the yellow grass. Gull pads. Gull probes. Gull stamps his feet. Gull whinnies up. Gull screams, tears, Pete tears, digs, Pete cuts, breaks, Pete stretches the corpse, flaps his wings, Pete's beak grows, probes, digs, pulls, the river jolts, no moon, what can I see. . . .

Mark lies, heavy, content, watches his smoke in the window, times his puff out, his hand falls (*with growing disgust*), smiles at absent guests, sucks in all comers, arranges his web, lies there a spider.[64]

In a subsequent conversation with Mark, Len tries to question him, but he has as little success as with Pete. Important questions like "Do you believe in God?" are by-passed until Len forces the point:

The point is, who are you. Not why or how, not even what. I can see what, perhaps, clearly enough. But who are you? It's no use saying you know who you are just because you tell me you can fit your particular key into a particular slot which will only receive your particular key because that's not foolproof and certainly not conclusive. Just because you're inclined to make these statements of faith has nothing to do with me. It's not my business. Occasionally I believe I perceive a little of what you are but that's pure accident. Pure accident on both our parts, the perceived and the perceiver. It's nothing like an accident, it's deliberate, it's a joint pretense. We depend on these accidents, on these contrived accidents, to continue. It's not important then that it's conspiracy, or hallucination. What you are, or appear to be to me, or appear to be to you, changes so quickly, so horrifyingly, I certainly can't keep up with it, and I'm damn sure you can't either. But who you are I can't even begin to recognize, and sometimes I recognize it so wholly, so forcibly, I can't look, and how can I be certain of what I see? You have no number. Where am I to look, where am I to look, what is there to locate, so as to have some surety, to have some rest from this whole bloody racket? You're the scum of so many reflections. How many reflections? Whose reflections? Is that what you consist of? What scum does the tide leave? What happens to the scum? When does it happen? I've seen what happens. But I can't speak when I see it. I can only point a finger. I can't even do that. The scum is broken and sucked back. I don't see where it goes. I don't see when, what do I see, what have I seen? What have I seen, the scum or the essence? What about it?[65]

But Mark is unmoved by these questions about personality until his vanity is pricked when, accidentally or deliberately, Len lets slip that Pete thinks that Mark is a fool. After this incident, Len is visited in a hospital by Mark and Pete, who are clearly at odds with each other while, at the same time, realizing that in some curious way they need each other. When Len comes out of the hospital, the dwarfs are preparing to leave him, and at the end of the play have left. So also, apparently, have Pete and Mark. The yard is clean and bare:

Now all is bare. All is clean. All is scrubbed. There is a lawn. There is a shrub. There is a flower.[66]

This clean, bare world seems to be redeemed by a flower, but we have no reason to suppose that the flower is any more real or less real than the previous garbage.

XV   *Critical Reaction to* The Dwarfs

The critics of the stage production of *The Dwarfs* certainly seem to have been bemused by it when Pinter produced it with *The Lover* in 1963. The difficulties in staging a radio play are always interesting, but even more so was the critical response to this repeat performance of the two plays, for neither was being seen for the first time, and both were in print. What the critics thought of the plays in this context becomes a fair test of their abilities. Drama critics in England do not have the same power to make or break a play that, we are told, New York critics have; nevertheless, it is unfortunately true that there is some relationship between their fiats and the success of a play. In this particular double bill, the easier play to hear, watch, and write about, *The Lover*, inevitably predominated in reviews; but, with the exception of *The New Statesman*, which simply gave a garbled version of the plot in two lines, most reviewers tackled *The Dwarfs* honorably as far as the number of lines given to it.

David Nathan, in the *Daily Herald* on September 19, 1963, wrote: "There came a point when I decided I had not got the password to Mr. Pinter's private though poetic world. Shortly afterwards I lost even the wish to enter it, and dreamed my own dreams while waiting passively for the curtain to fall." In varying degrees of agreement with Nathan are ranged the critics of *The Daily Telegraph*, *The Guardian*, *The Spectator*, *Punch*, and even Harold Hobson in *The Sunday Times*. The critic of *The Times* (September 20, 1963) connected both plays with an "incurable obsession with the elusiveness of reality" and out-Pintered Pinter with his final comment: "The resolution of the play comes when Len discovers a flower in his backyard: an undeniable object."

T. C. Worsley in *The Financial Times* seems to have been right when he suggested that the play demanded more of an audience, including critics, than the average one was prepared to give. But he suggested that there was a reward in listening to the "heightened prose of a quite remarkable quality." He also pointed out that the play was not quite adjusted to the stage, a point raised in *The Observer* by Bamber Gascoigne, who found the images muffled and blurred. Taylor, however, in *Plays and*

Players (November, 1963), felt that the transfer from radio to stage had come off better than one could have hoped because of the density of writing and the switches from subjective to objective moods. For a critic, Taylor offered an unusual conclusion: "The result is that one does not finally care about whether the play is or is not in theory 'theatrical'; it is a riveting experience in the theater, and that, after all, is what really counts." *Tot homines, tot veritates!*

But the play was by no means new, and, even if it had been, it is the job of a critic to express an opinion that will guide those people who have to pay for their tickets. We have a right to expect, even in a daily newspaper, more than a brief glance at the plot or a tentative foray into symbolic logic. Most of those reviewers who recognized that the play was "poetic" failed to give the language the attention such recognition necessitates. It is fascinating, for example, to speculate on the "bullock" image, one drawn from *A Slight Ache* and used again in the second play on the bill, *The Lover*. The language of *The Dwarfs* is undeniably less vernacular, and, of all Pinter's plays, seems to suggest foreign influence. Kitchin remarked on the coincidence between *The Dwarfs* and the crabs in Sartre's *Altona* (1959): ". . . there is the feeling that this is tapping a big continental thing, and not just a parochial, though you bring it . . . you make it English that for me is a pleasure . . . you absolutely digest it."[67]

This Englishness is crucial, but the work of Sartre's that springs to mind is surely *Nausea*. And we would do well in this context to take Iris Murdoch's advice on the interpretation of *Nausea*: "The rich overabundance of reality, the phantasmagoria of 'disordered' sensation, seem to the author of *La Nausée* a horrifying rather than a releasing spectacle, a threat to the possibility of meaning and truth. The more surprising contents of our consciousness are to be interpreted as distorted versions of our deep intentions and *not as dependent symbols* [italics mine], and certainly not as strays from a subterranean region of supreme power and value. Sartre fears, not loves, this notion of a volcanic otherness within the personality."[68] What we have to do is analyze the ambiguity that we hear.

Transferring the play from radio to stage solved certain problems that radio imposed: the stage production makes clear which speeches are soliloquy and which are monologues with Pete or

Mark present. Pinter's production also cleared up Taylor's difficulty over the end of the play. Taylor, who compared Len with Aston in *The Caretaker*, suggested that Len still has Aston's desperate remedy to come, hovering as he is on the brink of mental insanity: ". . . when we leave him [he] is perhaps already in a mental home."[69] (Or is he? It depends whether Pete is being evasive when he says that Len is in hospital suffering from 'kidney' trouble, or simply stating a fact.) Pinter's production showed the last speech spoken by a Len discharged from the hospital and back home (cured?)—a fact that may color the interpretation of the last speech and which certainly seemed to me to offer an upward shift; for the play is a kind of poem in which the images do a great deal of work.

XVI   *The Meaning of* The Dwarfs

Pete and Mark are straight Pinter characters—inconsequential in conversation, they avoid real communication or real questions as much as possible. Both gull and spider are, in their different ways, scavengers, predators feeding on corpses. They shun the truth to the point of ignoring Len's unusual behavior until Mark's vanity is pricked. Each thinks, or says, that the other is bad for Len. Len, as the central character, is, therefore, the most interesting. He seems to be nearly mad and reminds us of what we assume Aston, in *The Caretaker*, must have been like before his operation. We are, for once, taken into Len's mind (the advantage of a radio production, of course, but a new venture for Pinter); and yet, the ultimate question remains, as in *A Slight Ache*: who are you?

This question of verification has shifted in *The Dwarfs* from the audience to the plot of the play; the characters themselves want to know. And whether they want to understand or refuse to do so, the result is the same: will people tell the truth about themselves, and, if they genuinely want to, can they? Pinter has described his characters as people at the extreme edge of their being, where they live very much alone.[70] We ordinarily presume that beneath the spurious permanency naming confers upon objects, there is a more absolute kind of permanency, what Miss Murdoch calls "a subterranean region of supreme power and value"—but is there?

In Pinter's plays of this period, we get *inside* two people: Aston, in *The Caretaker*, who allows himself to be totally known, possibly because after the operation there is nothing to know; and Len. And, Taylor has pointed out, the more we learn about Len, and the more he tells us, the less we know. Both total objectivity and total subjectivity are useless: at one end of the scale, there are no motives, and all is mysterious; at the other, there are as many motives as possible, and the result is as mystifying as before. Martin Esslin has shown how the process of healing in Stanley, in Aston, and now in Len is also a catastrophe; it means the loss of a dimension in their lives, the dimension of fantasy and poetry, the ability to look behind the façade of the common, everyday world.[71] Pinter is dealing with characters trying to make the crucial adjustment that will make them members of society rather than outsiders. If they can adjust, there will be time for them to share in the games of society—for example, sex, as we shall see in *The Collection* and *The Lover*. Usually such characters do not succeed in making the adjustment, as is illustrated in Pinter's first successful long play, *The Caretaker*, which is about a room and the climactic moment in three people's lives. The isolation is also, we must remember, partly a deliberate device on the author's part: "We are only concerned with what is happening then, in this particular moment of these people's lives. There is no reason to suppose that at one time or another they did not listen at political meetings ... or that they haven't ever had girl friends."[72]

CHAPTER 3

The Caretaker

DISCUSSING *The Dwarfs* and the novel from which it was adapted, Bamber Gascoigne in *The Observer* remarked that the novel must have contained the seeds of Pinter's plays: "As in *The Caretaker*, three characters jockey for power over one another. The central character, Len, is pulled in one direction by the ferocious activity of Pete and in another by the indolent materialism of Mark. To escape their influence he withdraws defensively to his room, one of Pinter's favorite images. Like Stanley in *The Birthday Party*, Len is paranoic; like Aston in *The Caretaker* he ends up being straightened out in hospital, until his vision is neat, sterilised, normal." Such an interpretation is plausible, but the cure seems to me doubtful. And the doubt is of a different kind from that which must be felt in either *The Birthday Party* or in *The Caretaker*, in which Stanley and Aston are silenced. Len, on the other hand, may have acquired neat, clean vision, but it is attended by a lawn, a shrub and a flower, which have an imaginative pull that the dumbness of Stanley and the taciturnity of Aston cannot have. The link with *The Caretaker* is there, of course; and it is something more than mere chronology (*The Caretaker* appeared in April, *The Dwarfs* in December of 1960); they are both of a piece.

However, *The Dwarfs* has remained enigmatic and daunting to popular taste, while *The Caretaker*, in spite of a brief initial run, marks the beginning of Pinter's public recognition—a recognition, moreover, that has operated retrospectively to affect earlier plays previously rejected. Clifford Leech says that *The Caretaker* "seems now to be the most impressive dramatic writing in English since the war, but we cannot know if he will go beyond it, we cannot know how even this play will look if there is a future from which it may be regarded."[1] Laurence Kitchin sees it as the peak of English compressionistic drama: "Within his formula, *The Caretaker* is so perfectly constructed that it

would be an impertinence to advocate further lessons in crafts-
manship; and the foreign influences are thrown off both in
characterization and dialogue. Better still, there are allusions to
a wider context, to the affluent society's materialism and cruelty
to its casualties."[2]

As far as Pinter himself is concerned, the play is simply a
logical extension of his basic idea with nothing very difficult
about it: "I went into a room and saw one person standing up
and one person sitting down, and a few weeks later I wrote *The
Room*. I went into another room and saw two people sitting
down, and a few years later [?] I wrote *The Birthday Party*. I
looked through a door into a third room, and saw two people
standing up and I wrote *The Caretaker*."[3] But the play has invited complex responses. When Terence Rattigan saw it as an
allegory about the God of the Old Testament, the God of the
New Testament, and Humanity, Pinter replied that the play was
about a caretaker and two brothers; and so it is. It also, as a play,
marks the end of violence and of the triumph of violence that
has been modified progressively from *The Room* onward. In *The
Caretaker*, violence becomes the practical jokes played by Mick
on Davies (Mick is well named since he does "take the Mick"
out of Davies!):

Harold Pinter's ability to construct in depth is even greater, his range
of vernacular dialogue wider than Wesker's, the social comment less
explicit. Pinter began by using shock tactics, derived from Kafka,
Ionesco and Hemingway, to activate wittily observed behavior. Sup-
porters unhelpfully stressed the gimmicks, detractors the resultant obscurity. But Pinter has been relegating violence to its proper place,
off-stage; whereas *The Room*, in his first play, exhibited the beating
of a blind negro, Aston in *The Caretaker* describes a ghastly experience calmly, in one long speech. Not photographic, since the diction
is exuberantly pepped up, *The Caretaker* is naturalistic all the same.
Its action a conflict of illusions, is like Gorki material worked over by
Chekhov.[4]

Pinter's achievement here, surely, is that he combines social
commentary with Absurd Theater. Esslin is right when he
sees Aston and Mick as exemplars of the "do-it-yourself," mid-
twentieth-century species of Western man seeking security in
expertise.[5]

[88]

Originally, violence was intended as the resolution of the play:
"At the end of *The Caretaker*, there are two people alone in a
room, and one of them must go in such a way as to produce a
sense of complete separation and finality. I thought originally
that the play must end with the violent death of one at the hands
of the other. But then I realised, when I got to the point, that
the characters as they had grown could never act in this way."[6]
In his interview with Tynan, Pinter was more explicit: "The
original idea was to end the play with the violent death of the
tramp. It suddenly struck me that it was not necessary. And I
think that in this play I have developed, that I have no need to
use cabaret turns and blackouts and screams in the dark to the
extent that I enjoyed using them before. I feel that I can deal,
without resorting to that kind of thing, with a human situation.
I do see this play as merely a particular human situation, concerning three particular people, and not, incidentally, symbols."[7]

The play is not without its symbolism, however. It opens in a
shabby room cluttered with junk (including the kitchen sink)
where the steady drip of water from the leaky roof into a bucket
functions very much like the faulty toilet in *The Dumb Waiter*.

I *The Action of the Play*

When *The Caretaker* begins, a young man in his late twenties
named Mick, wearing a leather jacket, is surveying the room.
When he hears voices approaching the room, he leaves, and
Aston, a man in his early thirties, enters, accompanied by a tramp
who calls himself MacDavies (betraying a mixed Scottish-Welsh
ancestry?) and whom Aston has just rescued from a fight in a
café. Aston, a slow-witted but kind man, offers Davies a bed for
the night. Davies, in his rambling talk, very quickly emerges as
an opinionated, narrow-minded, prejudiced, irascible old lay-
about whose perpetual talk contrasts sharply with Aston's taciturnity; and his talkativeness is, as in *A Slight Ache*, partly
fostered by Aston's silence.

Davies's conversation, whether we believe it or not, tells us of
his employment in the café where he was "put on" by the colored
customers; of his hatred of dirt (he left his wife a fortnight after
marriage ostensibly because he found her dirty underwear in the
vegetable pan!); of his hatred of Blacks, Greeks, and Poles—and

particularly Blacks; of his feeling that the world owes him a living, particularly a pair of shoes—if we do not believe the story
of the monastery at Luton, we do see the necessity for good
shoes; and of his habit, even in circumstances of beggary, of
being choosy.

Thus, the shoes that Aston offers him in the play are usually
the wrong color, the wrong shape, the wrong size, or the wrong
material; or they have no shoelaces; or the shoelaces offered are
the wrong color for the shoes—details that, in Davies's homeless,
shabby condition, seem ludicrously insisted upon. Davies is not
merely homeless, he has even lost his identity and has been using
the name of Jenkins for years. To prove who he really is, he
would have to go down to Sidcup to get his papers, assuming
that there really are papers there. Of course, he never *can* get
down to Sidcup—either the weather is wrong, or the shoes are
wrong, etc. Aston, on the other hand, likes to work with his
hands, wants to clear the garden and build a shed, and can only
drink Guinness from a thin glass. He collects junk almost compulsively, the central piece of which is a Buddha, chosen, again,
because it is well made.

From the first night, it is obvious that these two men will not
be able to live in harmony. The tramp Davies keeps Aston awake
at night with his jabbering and dreams, both of which he angrily
denies in the morning and attributes to the Blacks next door. On
the other hand, Davies is uneasy in the room full of junk, be-
wildered by Aston's references to machines—to a jig saw,[8] to
plugging in the electric fire, to learning to use the vacuum cleaner—and even apprehensive of the gas stove, although it is not
connected to the mains. Aston's conversation, such as it is, is not
easy to follow. He can move from the discussion of some new
tool he hopes to pick up to the story of a woman in a café who
wanted to have a look at his body. Davies makes suggestions
about finding work, but he is quite content to do nothing. As
soon as Aston leaves, he begins to poke about the flat, trying to
find some meaning (financial value) in the accumulated junk.
As he does this, Mick re-enters and throws him to the floor with
the brisk question: "What's the game?"

In Act Two, a few seconds later, the trouserless Davies is still
on the floor, but Mick is transformed into a smoothly polite, very
friendly Cockney who is glad to hear that Davies slept well and

who is awfully glad to meet him. Mick's conversation, rapid and fluent, is as frightening to Davies as Aston's silence. Mick, who insists on identifying poor Davies with someone else, shows at the same time a baffling knowledge of London:

You know, believe it or not, you've got a funny kind of resemblance to a bloke I once knew in Shoreditch. Actually he lived in Aldgate. I was staying with a cousin in Camden Town. This chap, he used to have a pitch in Finsbury Park, just by the bus depot. When I got to know him I found out he was brought up in Putney. That didn't make any difference to me. I know quite a few people who were born in Putney. Even if they weren't born in Putney they were born in Fulham. The only trouble was, he wasn't born in Putney, he was only brought up in Putney. It turned out he was born in the Caledonian Road, just before you get to the Nag's Head. His old mum was still living at the Angel. All the buses passed right by the door. She could get a 38, 581, 30 or 38A, take her down the Essex Road to Dalston Junction in next to no time. Well, of course, if she got the 30 he'd take her up Upper Street way, round Highbury Corner and down to St. Paul's Church, but she'd get to Dalston Junction just the same in the end. I used to leave my bike in her garden on my way to work. Yes, it was a curious affair. Dead spit of you he was. Bit bigger round the nose but there was nothing in it.[9]

All this detail simply adds to the vagueness surrounding Davies himself. What is worse, not only does Mick insist on confusing him with other people, but he also tells Davies that the house belongs to him, and the room, and even the bed Davies slept in, which he offers to sell for a fair price. This bargain is interrupted only by the return of Aston with a bag of things for Davies. After a piece of byplay with this bag between the two brothers and poor Davies (strongly reminiscent of the scene with Lucky's hat in *Waiting for Godot*), Mick leaves, and Aston, explaining nothing except that Mick is his brother and has a sense of humor, offers Davies the job of caretaker when the room has been decorated. Davies, reasonably enough in the circumstances, is evasive, particularly about answering inquiries at the door and about having his name on a card:

Of course I got plenty of other cards lying about, but they don't know that and I can't tell them, can I, because then they'd find out I was going about under an assumed name. You see, the name I call myself now, that's not my real name. My real name's not the one I'm using, you see. It's different. You see, the name I go under now ain't my real one. It's assumed.[10]

This scene fades. The next one begins with the entry of Davies into a darkened room where the lights will not work and where a figure begins to hunt him with a vacuum cleaner. Suddenly the light goes on, and Mick plausibly explains that he has been doing a bit of spring cleaning. Mick offers the frightened, rather hostile Davies a sandwich and begins to confide in him by asking his advice, for, he says, Davies is a man of the world. First, Mick introduces the subject of his brother, Aston, who is funny (although Mick, ominously, turns sharply on Davies when Davies agrees that he is); second, the decorating of the house, which will then need a caretaker. Assured that Davies has references at Sidcup, Mick offers him the job and leaves; and, in the next scene, Davies, beginning to feel confident and powerful from these discoveries (and quite overlooking Mick's changeable moods), begins to quibble with Aston about his bed and the window.

Aston, however, is not really listening. Half to the tramp and half to himself, he speaks of the time in his life when he used to see things very clearly, talk to people, and mix with them, until one day he was sent to a hospital for examination. There the doctor told him that he was ill and that something would have to be done to his mind so that he could go out and "live like the others." When his mother gave permission for this treatment, he tried to escape; and, when he was caught, he tried to prevent the shock treatment by standing up—but the shock was administered anyway, and he went home. But his thoughts had become slow and uncertain, and he could not move his head or write any more:

And I laid everything out, in order, in my room all the things I knew were mine, but I didn't die. I never had those hallucinations any more. And I never spoke to anyone any more. The funny thing is, I can't remember much . . . about what I said, what I thought . . . I mean before I went into that place. The thing is I should have been dead. I should have died. And then, anyway, after a time, I got a bit better, and I started to do things with my hands, and then about two years ago I came here, because my brother had got this house and so I decided to have a go at decorating it, so I came into this room, and I started to collect wood, for my shed, and all these bits and pieces, that I thought might come in handy for the flat, or around the house, sometime. I feel much better now. But I don't talk to people now. I steer clear of places like that cafe. I never go into them now. I don't talk to anyone . . . like that. I've often thought of going back and trying to find the man who did that to me. But I want to do something first. I want to build that shed out in the garden.[11]

The sad truth is that Aston *has* talked as he used to, confidingly. Also, the consequence of the operation is that he can only put things into their proper places and that he has lost curiosity. In this respect, he reminds us of Len (who tries to put things in order, but remains curious) or Edward.

Two weeks later, Davies, confident of his position in the room, talks quite openly to Mick about Aston's failings and encourages Mick to reveal his plans for turning the room into a luxury flat, a penthouse in the very latest style:

I'd have teal-blue, copper and parchment linoleum squares. I'd have those colors re-echoed in the walls. I'd offset the kitchen units with charcoal-grey worktops. Plenty of room for cupboards for the crockery. We'd have a small wall cupboard, a large wall cupboard, a corner wall cupboard with revolving shelves. You wouldn't be short of cupboards. You could put the dining-room across the landing, see? Yes. Venetian blinds, venetian blinds on the window, cork floor, cork tiles. You could have an off-white pile linen rug, a table in . . . in afromosia teak veneer, sideboard with matt black drawers, curved chairs with cushioned seats, armchairs in oatmeal tweed, beech frame settee with woven sea-grass seat, white-topped heat-resistant coffee table, white tile surround. Yes. Then the bedroom. What's a bedroom? It's a retreat. It's a place to go for rest and peace. So you want quiet decoration. The lighting functional. Furniture . . . mahogany and rosewood. Deep azure-blue carpet, unglazed blue and white curtains, a bedspread with a pattern of small blue roses on a white ground, dressing table with a lift-up top containing a plastic tray, table lamp of white raffia . . . (MICK *sits up*) it wouldn't be a flat it'd be a palace.[12]

But Davies is not even listening to Mick's dream. He presses on with his own demands—a clock to tell the time by, for example—principally, that Mick should speak to his brother, who is disturbing Davies at night and annoying him. But, when Aston comes in, Mick disappears as usual. The shoes that Aston produces are not satisfactory, and Aston wakes Davies that night because he is making noises. Davies, annoyed at being wakened in the middle of the night, taunts Aston with the memory of the hospital:

They can put them pincers on your head again, man! They can have them on again! Any time. All they got to do is get the word. They'd carry you in there, boy. They'd come here and pick you up and carry you in! They'd keep you fixed! They'd put them pincers on your head, they'd have you fixed! They'd take one look at all this junk I got to sleep with they'd know you were a creamer. That was the greatest mistake they made, you take my tip, letting you get out of that place. . . .[13]

When Aston quietly tells Davies that he had better go, he plays his trump card—Mick's offer of a job as caretaker. It will be Aston who has to go. Aston firmly puts him out, defeating Davies's attempted violence.

The next scene shows Davies and Mick. Mick is smooth and polite, but he points out immediately that Davies does get a bit out of his depth. Davies now finds that he is expected to be an interior decorator. He denies this, insisting that Mick must have the wrong man. But Mick replies: "How could I have the wrong man? You're the only man I've spoken to. You're the only man I've told, about my dreams, about my deepest wishes, you're the only one I've told, and I only told you because I understood you were an experienced first-class professional interior and exterior decorator."[14]

And, when Davies calls Aston "nutty," Mick turns on Davies and dismisses him:

What a strange man you are. Aren't you? You're really strange. Ever since you come into this house there's been nothing but trouble. Honest. I can take nothing you say at face value. Every word you speak is open to any number of different interpretations. Most of what you say is lies. You're violent, you're erratic, you're just completely unpredictable. You're nothing else but a wild animal, when you come down to it. You're a barbarian. And to put the old tin lid on it, you stink from arse-hole to breakfast time. Look at it. You come here recommending yourself as an interior decorator, whereupon I take you on, and what happens? You make a long speech about all the references you've got down at Sidcup, and what happens? I haven't noticed you go down to Sidcup to obtain them. It's all most regrettable but it looks as though I'm compelled to pay you off for your caretaking work. Here's half a dollar.[15]

Then, in a fit of anger, Mick washes his hands of the house and smashes the Buddha on the floor as Aston enters. The brothers do not speak, but smile faintly at each other, and Mick leaves.[16] Davies now tries to reconcile himself with Aston, but fails, and the play ends with Davies's pathetic reference to the papers at Sidcup, which, like the promise of Faustus to burn his books, fails.

II   *What the Play Is About*

The play is apparently about two brothers who deliberately confide their dreams in Davies, either because they ironically believe such a confidence will be safe or because they know it will be betrayed. Davies cannot resist playing off one brother against the other, until they unite and kindly, but firmly, throw him out. In spite of its serious theme, the play is extremely rich in comedy. Leonard Russell in *The Sunday Times* was upset by an audience that laughed at it as if it were a Whitehall farce. Pinter answered this point in a letter published on August 14, 1960:

Certainly I laughed myself while writing "The Caretaker" but not all the time, not "indiscriminately." An element of the absurd is, I think, one of the features of the play, but at the same time I did not intend it to be merely a laughable farce. If there hadn't been other issues at stake the play would not have been written.

Audience reaction can't be regulated, and no one would want it to be; nor is it easy to analyse. But where the comic and the tragic (for want of a better word) are closely interwoven, certain members of an audience will always give emphasis to the comic as opposed to the other, for by so doing they rationalize the other out of existence.

Pinter regards this indiscriminate laughter as a kind of smoke screen the audience throws up to protect itself, and he dissociates himself from it: "As far as I am concerned, 'The Caretaker' is funny, up to a point. Beyond that point it ceases to be funny, and it was because of that point that I wrote it." The laughter at this play is obviously qualified.

As the unreliability and unworthiness of Davies appear, the characters of the two brothers are also brought out, and our sympathies are constantly shifting. Aston has his pathetic dream of building a hut in the garden and the awful history of his treatment in a lunatic asylum,[17] while Mick has an equally pathetic dream of turning his dilapidated slum into a luxury flat. And Davies has his dream of papers in Sidcup. Although the two brothers rarely speak—indeed they are rarely on the stage together—they seem to communicate without words; and each protects the other in his own way. Davies, much as he needs a place in the world—even in a junk-filled room—cannot behave as a caretaker, and his failure to do so is a kind of *hubris*. The surprising thing is that in spite of his total worthlessness, we find it possible to feel sympathy for him at the end of the play.

The organizing factor is once more the dialogue, which moves easily from completely naturalistic talk into fantasy, producing contrasts between verbosity and taciturnity, both evasions in the fearful matter of communication. On all sides, the question asked is still: what or who am I? There is no sex except for the briefly related episode of Aston's encounter with the woman in the café, no social life, although Mick must go somewhere in his van, and Aston did pick Davies up in a café, and no politics except for Davies's extreme racist views. There are no ideas even. There are simply people living very much alone.

III *The Film of* The Caretaker

The film, renamed *The Guest* in America, made with Donald Pleasance and Alan Bates from the original cast and Robert Shaw replacing Peter Woodthorpe as Aston,[18] removes some of the ambiguities; but, sensitively directed by Clive Donner, it remains a Pinter play. It is, in fact, the work of a magnificently dedicated and integrated team. Shot on location at Hackney for the ridiculously low sum of £30,000 without guarantee of distribution—it was financed privately with a list of backers ranging from Noel Coward and Elizabeth Taylor to the continuity girl —it was shown at the Edinburgh Festival and later at the Academy Cinema in London. The earliest critical notice was by

The Caretaker

Mordecai Richler in *Town* (December, 1963), who found it a curiously bothersome film: "There are some delightful conversational turns from Pinter, a dialogue about old shoes and monks in Luton, another exchange about a caretaker's implements, but I was left with the feeling of being tricked, taken, the way years ago Cocteau (in his fashion) used to con audiences with effects. I thought the obscurity was not inherent in what Pinter had to say but essential to conceal the absence of core to *The Caretaker*. In short, shot upon significant shot of the Buddha statue, I still felt I was being artily had. However, I should add I'm in a minority."

That he *was* in a minority proved true when the film was shown in London. Penelope Gilliatt in *The Observer* (March 14, 1964) observed that the tramp is "haunted by suspicions of malevolence, but he has no one to ask about them; so when he is talked to he often says 'What?,' not because he hasn't heard, but as a hopeless way of gaining time and puzzling out how much ground he has just lost." She wondered how dramatists had managed to do without this style of dialogue for so long and praised the whole film unreservedly. Dilys Powell in *The Sunday Times* (March 15, 1964) was equally impressed, and she saw the film as having a simple plot but as being *about* three solitaries in a claustrophobic room. Her comment that the tramp also has his fantasy (belonging to everyday life in terms of having a pair of shoes, re-establishing his identity in terms of papers at Sidcup) was pertinent; and, as she remarked, though funny, the film is about very serious matters—solitude, ingratitude, and cruelty.

John Coleman in *The New Statesman* (March 13, 1964) also praised the film as a remarkably professional job—one very well done on a low budget. He sees Mick's motive in getting rid of the tramp not so much as resulting from annoyance at being deceived as from a desire to protect his brother—a very plausible interpretation of the film version. Coleman suggested that the film was more satisfying than the play because it touched the audience on the raw, in its fury, as he put it, "with the whole devious business of clambering over the minds of one's fellow men in search of some local self-aggrandisement." Isabel Quigly, in *The Spectator* (March 20, 1964) was similarly impressed, but she felt that the brothers threw the old man out simply because

they were tired of his "nasty and obtrusive presence," an interpretation that has the virtue of simplicity as well as backing from
Pleasance's portrayal.

Critics, on the whole, were impressed with actors, author, producer, and the work of the cameraman, Nicolas Roeg. The content of their criticism showed more competency, elegance, and
expertise than most drama critics have shown so far when dealing with Pinter. As John Cutts wrote in *Films and Filming* (January, 1964), one can take one's pick in *The Caretaker* of a half
dozen allegories, but too severe rationalization gets in the way
of enjoying the ambiguity and contradictions that make it a film
that is "funny, accurate, poignant, provocative, and, at all times,
unique."

IV   *From Play into Film*

Pinter and Donner discussed the film in an article published
in the summer of 1963.[19] In it, they raised the three points any
such translation from stage to film must involve: was the play
cinematic; did the film open the play out; and did that opening
out lead to the inclusion of life outside—that exterior always
projected, never denied, but apparently contradicted by the
claustrophobic atmosphere and theme of the play? The three
points are really facets of the same subject. Pinter suggested that
the situation must basically be cinematic: "It seemed to me, that
when you have two people standing on the stairs and one asks
the other if he would like to be caretaker in this house, and the
other bloke, you know, who is work-shy doesn't want in fact to
say no, he doesn't want the job, but at the same time he wants to
edge it around. . . . Now it seems to me there's an enormous
amount of internal conflict within one of the characters and
external conflict between them—and it's exciting cinema."

Clearly, some difference in the treatment is inevitable, since a
film is not confined to a picture-stage as the play was: "You
can say the play has been 'opened out' in the sense that things
I'd yearned to do, without knowing it, in writing for the stage,
crystallised when I came to think about it as a film. Until then
I didn't know that I wanted to do them because I'd accepted
the limitations of the stage. For instance, there's a scene in the
garden of the house, which is very silent; two silent figures with
a third looking on. I think in the film one has been able to hit

the relationship of the brothers more clearly than in the play." In being able to move outside the room, the film established the outside world as a reality in contact with the room:

What I'm very pleased about myself is that in the film, as opposed to the play, we see a real house and real snow outside, dirty snow and the streets. We don't see them very often but they're there, the backs of houses and windows, attics in the distance. There is actually sky as well, a dirty one, and these characters move in the context of a real world—as I believe they do. In the play, when people were confronted with just a set, a room and a door, they often assumed it was all taking place in limbo, in a vacuum, and the world outside hardly existed, or had existed at some point but was only half remembered. Now one thing which I think is triumphantly expressed in the film is Clive's concentration on the characters when they are outside the room, outside the house. Not that there aren't others. There are others. There are streets, there is traffic, shadows, shapes about, but he is for me concentrating on the characters as they walk, and while we go into the world outside it is almost as if only these characters exist.

All three points in fact become one: the art of transferring a stage play into the essentially naturalistic medium of the cinema.

Pinter was asked elsewhere whether or not this "opening out" did not alter the play:

No. You see, when . . . the thing about the play is that a certain number of . . . body of people consider that as it was all in a particular room on the stage, that it was taking place in a limbo, in a vacuum and there wasn't any world outside now I always felt . . . I had no opportunity in the limitations of the stage to state this . . . except in the program note which I can't write you see, I mean program notes . . . that there is a world outside. I felt there should be anyway taken for granted that for some odd reason they wanted got the devil and . . . materialism and . . . mankind and God and Christ you know as . . . as these characters which I understand them then it got . . . got taken out of its natural place which was a room in a house in a street in a town in the world, so I was very glad of the opportunity to go outside and just show that people did come in, when they came in the door they had come in from the street you know and also there was a garden when in the play the man said . . . Aston the elder brother said . . . "all that wood under that tarpaulin in the yard" when given there to build his shed, there was wood under a tarpaulin.[20]

Thus, as Pinter points out, we actually see Mick's van, a real van in a real street. The film, therefore, removes at least one ambiguity: "it seems to me the core of our living, you know, this ambiguity. But the ambiguity I would prefer to do without the . . . wasn't ambiguous to me but it was ambiguous to a certain proportion of the audience as to whether there is a van outside so you understand for instance whether there is such a place as the café on the corner do you know. Not that we ever go to the café on the corner but in fact just to underline quite delicately I think that these men do move outside and come back to the room, that's all I meant."

In fact, we see Mick breakfasting at the café round the corner. The film in this one important respect is clearer. The assumption of the audience that the play takes place in a kind of vacuum, is, of course, a kind of triumph of theme over decor, since audiences never question the presence of the garden in, for example, *Hedda Gabler,* though they usually do not see it. The interpolations in the film—street scenes, a visit to a secondhand clothes shop, the garden scenes with a coffin-shaped fish pond, even breakfast in a café with Mick—do not alter the basic fidelity of the film to the original play. And there is one superb addition to replace the curtain that falls after Aston's long and harrowing speech. This new scene breaks the tension without destroying the emotion. Davies, sitting on a roadside bench, is picked up by the ebullient Mick in his van and threatened with a visit to Sidcup. The horror this suggestion arouses is immediately dissipated in laughter as Mick solemnly drives the tramp round a traffic island, deposits him where he found him, and makes excuses about the heavy traffic and shortage of gas.

The greatest danger of filming the play, since it relies as drama very much on dialogue, is that whereas in the theater people do listen fairly attentively, in the cinema, many effects are achieved too glibly and too visually. Indeed, the adaptation is acute in recognizing what the cinema does and does not require. As Taylor pointed out, the additions, largely of wordless exteriors, "have the proper effect of emphasizing the intensity and isolation of the scenes in the room, rather than breaking the concentration."[21] The additions help, therefore, to locate the play.

V   *The Meaning of* The Caretaker

What the play means, obviously, depends upon the interpretation of the three characters, and particularly of Davies, even though he is far from being as sympathetic a center as Len in *The Dwarfs*. For *The Caretaker*—if we are still working in the private mythology of Pinter—is at a level where comprehensible motivation is available should we insist on it. Taylor interprets the play as follows. Mick is trying to get through to his brother, interest him in something. Davies is the first human being who has interested Aston since Aston left the mental home, and Mick, his jealousy aroused, wants to get rid of him. Mick realizes he can only do so if Aston voluntarily rejects Davies, and so he leads Davies into believing he will hire him as caretaker when the house is redecorated. Davies falls into the trap by trying to play off one brother against the other, by rejecting his real friend, Aston, for Mick, even going so far as telling Mick his brother is mad. Mick now rejects Davies, who tries to become reconciled with Aston, but it is too late. Aston has now determined to build his shed, and there is no place in his life for Davies, who has to leave as the curtain falls.[22]

This interpretation, however, seems to lay too much stress on motive, and, overlooking Mick's own dreams and insecurity, it makes him too much a villain and opportunist—and Davies too little of either. Nor is it true, as Taylor suggests, that only Davies is subject in his conversation to characteristic Pinter ambiguity. Certainly, Davies is trying to cover up his tracks and keep people guessing (we have no way of knowing whether there are papers at Sidcup or not)—but this is a theme as well as a method. Pinter defended a play written like this in his program note for the Royal Court production:

The desire for verification is understandable, but cannot always be satisfied. There are no hard distinctions between what is real and what is unreal, nor between what is true and what false. The thing is not necessarily either true or false; it can be both true and false. The assumption that to verify what has happened and what is happening presents few problems, I take to be inaccurate. A character on the stage who can present no convincing argument or information as to his past experiences, his present behavior or his aspirations, nor give a comprehensive analysis of his motives is as legitimate and as worthy of attention as one who, alarmingly, can do all these things. The more acute the experience, the less articulate its expression.

When Taylor says that only with Davies is there difficulty, he surely overlooks the fact that, for example, when Aston tells us why he is as he is, more questions are raised than answered. Further, we do not know Mick's game at all. But, as Taylor points out, whether or not our information about Davies is true is not very important (whereas we would like to know what Stanley had done, or who the blind Negro is, or even what the matchseller is). All we need to know, which is amply evidenced in the play, is that Davies is shifty and unreliable and probably incapable of telling the truth if he wanted to: ". . . his evasions and contradictions imply a judgment on him, but not necessarily the world around him."[24]

As John Arden suggests in his review of the play,[25] the story is a perfectly straightforward one, but the treatment of it is only near-conventional. Arden describes this Pinter method as one of writing with the corners never quite joined up: the inconsistencies are there, but never absolutely contradictory: "Thus, the elder brother's account of his brain-operation is highly detailed and circumstantial. But is it true? If it is true, why isn't Mr. Pinter writing a serious social play to denounce the cruelty prevalent in mental hospitals? And if it *isn't* true, why does it take the crucial place in the text, the climax of Act Two?" These are decidedly John Arden questions, and they inquire into the motives behind a play by Arden; and he concedes that they are impertinent because they are based on old ideas of realism. Irrelevance and pauses are exciting characteristics of *The Caretaker* and the "not-quiteness" is as carefully constructed as any situation or style in a so-called well-made play:

I do not think we should feel bound to look for any allegorical interpretations—they may be there: but there are no clues as to how to find them. Therefore any such search is surely more of a parlor game than serious literary appreciation. Taken purely at its face value this play is a study of the unexpected strength of family ties against an intruder. That in itself is a subject deep enough to carry many layers of meaning without our having to superimpose any extra scheme of

Symbols. It also, by its verbal patterns alone, tells us a great deal that is uncomfortable about the workings of the English mind today. So much of everything we see and hear is "never quite" anything. Never completely dreary but. . . .

The urge to allegorize is of course reasonable. In a sense, any meaning wrested from the play depends upon attaching labels to the characters and situations in order, ultimately, to make the play into an equation. And, if the urge were not irresistible, the central character, Davies, is a questionable moral quantity whatever the play may be saying. Sometimes a critic sees the play as part of a developing line of ideas and is encouraged to do so by Pinter's almost compulsive, yet modified, re-use of material. For example, Ruby Cohn sees the first four plays as being about virtual annihilation—and the curtain falls in *The Caretaker* on a poor old man's pleas to remain in his refuge.[26] She later refers to Davies as a "broken old man," as the defenseless victim of the System. Although she is willing to concede that he is the least sympathetic of victims, he is still crushed by the usual representatives of the System: Goldberg and McCann, then Ben and Gus, and now Aston and Mick (Aston = Carpenter/Christ + Mick = leather jacket/van).

For Cohn, Pinter's villains descend from motorized vans to close in on their victims in stuffy rooms. The system they represent is as stuffy and shabby as the room, and we cannot, as in Osborne's realistic drama, marry into it, sneak into it, or rave against it in self-expressive anger. The essence of a Pinter victim is final, inarticulate helplessness: ". . . instead of allowing the old man to die beaten, the System insists on tantalising him with faint hope, thereby immeasurably increasing his final desperate anguish. There is perhaps a pun contained in the title: the Caretaker is twisted into a taker on of care, for care is the human destiny."

This seems willful and perverse as an interpretation. Reading the text, it may be possible to feel sorry for Davies, but Pleasance's dirty, servile, cruel presence on the stage actively prevents this sympathy from getting out of hand. And what of the sadness of Mick? And, if we must read through the plays in sequence, what of the crucial operation on Aston that links him with Stanley and Len? We could, for example, pursue the Christ

image in Aston and Len. Kay Dick also reads the plays in sequence and sees *The Caretaker* as the final triumph, after an
exploration of violence (Mick) that fails, of passive resistance
(Aston).[27] But such an interpretation linguistically, and presumably morally, implies that the shock treatment cure was a
good thing—society's way of building Aston up. The principle
dramatic objection to this is the great pain Aston's description
causes. Moreover, however sympathetic a character Aston is, his
present condition is near simple-mindedness. The shifting sympathies of the audience are at once the virtue and the vice of the
play: the virtue, because they mirror the complexity of life; the
vice, because they lead back to subjective taste. Thus, there is a
variety of attitudes among critics who sympathize with Davies.
For Wilson Knight, as might be expected, Davies is Dionysiac,
radiating lines of force and dignity from his vagabond personality:

The two brothers Aston and Mick are intelligent young men of some
education, but one has been in a mental home and the other appears
to be a near-candidate. They, especially Aston, and their general situation and prospects together with their extraordinary room, appear to
be peculiarly static: they are getting, and are likely to get, nowhere.
In contrast the tramp is dynamic; and it is natural that the mentally
paralysed Aston should welcome him to his home of meaningless
jumble. The disreputable Davies is baffled by the lumber, is afraid
of the stove, and finds draughts from the broken window more disturbing than the open roads. Two worlds, those of a vigorous outsider and those of a derelict civilisation, conflict.[28]

This raises a great number of questions. If Davies is so dynamic, why does he never get to Sidcup? And the window is not
broken; it is open because Aston hates confinement and stench.
Wilson Knight's tempting contrast between two kinds of personality—outsider and civilized man—overrules the play and
softens the character of Davies, who more resembles Dionysian
than Dionysus. Even the most sympathetic supporter of Davies
would agree that we do not enjoy being on his side. As Clifford
Leech writes:

We are invited, however repellent the prospect, to identify ourselves
with Davies; he is our representative as the central character in a
morality play is. Aston and Mick are individualizations of forces, war-

ring principles, dark angel and bright angel. They are brothers, and as they are together for a moment, in silence, near the end of the play, they smile faintly at one another. Between them there is understanding and affection, for they are of the same order, aristocrats in the universe: the principle of assertion, ruthlessness, mockery; the principle of suffering, love, compassion.[29]

Surely this again overlooks the insecurities of both Mick and Aston. The silence of the one and the loquaciousness of the other cover the same fear. Leech finally feels the play is Aston's tragedy because love has turned away. Moreover, on the stage, the two brothers do not strike us as characters from *Paradise Lost* but simply as two brothers such as we could meet in the street. Cosmic implications are out of place in *The Caretaker*; as Bamber Gascoigne pertinently reminds us, they should not be brought in with reminiscences of *Waiting for Godot*. Pinter's tramps do not discuss cosmic matters: "They merely fight about who shall sleep in which bed, or they make plans, or they grumble; and the play's interest comes directly from the way in which they do these things. At its best it is the very essence of naturalistic drama."[30] Davies is, after all, of the same kind as the brothers. He, too, has his dream, for the constant project of collecting his papers at Sidcup comes easily to represent "all human dreams of definite and responsible actions."

VI   *An Interpretation of* The Caretaker

Perhaps the fullest and most sympathetic treatment of the whole play and what it means has been provided by Boulton.[31] To him, the tramp Davies[32] is the archetypal symbol of life as a journey: "It is not introduced with the formality of Beckett in *Waiting for Godot* where one is always aware of its presence; rather the symbol is unobtrusively established by Davies's frequent references to his journeying." Further, this journey has no real purpose; it is not only a journey along an uncertain road, but one that is also friendless and terrifying. The sympathy aroused by the play is distributed: it is invited for Aston, whose security is menaced, and also for Davies, whose refuge is lost, although he is plainly the destructive agent. There is fear and menace on both sides—the visit to the monastery thus becomes an account of a man seeking sympathy because of fear of a hostile world.

Tricks are played on Davies by Mick; Davies is constantly watching Aston (pretending to be asleep when he is not, for example); and both brothers make Davies feel his isolation. Mick is actively suspicious, and Aston gradually grows aware of the threat to his existence.

On his part, Davies seeks pre-eminence and cannot be content. Thus, Aston's getting to the root of the trouble with the broken electric plug at the beginning of the play is an image of the problem of the whole play: *getting to the root of the trouble*. And the trouble here is catalyzed by the presence of Davies. Inevitably, Davies reveals natural human depravity. But the subject of the play is really the question of identity for all three characters, repeating the motif from *The Room* (the Negro's calling on Rose) and *The Birthday Party* (Stanley's plea that he is the same): Davies admits his pretences, but the identities of the two brothers are not much clearer. One lives elsewhere and owns a house that his brother lives in; and, in spite of the details amassed through the play, neither has a historical existence. Man, then, is a mystery and unknowable, making the play add up to: ". . . a view of man moving further and further from a questionable innocence associated with childhood to the treacherous and evil world of experience; at once pathetic and humorous, man becomes a status-seeker looking for acceptance and security in a world that is unpredictable and has to be fought on its own terms; and because innocence has been lost, man cannot trust his fellows, does not frankly reveal himself to them, perhaps does not honestly know himself." Of this state of affairs, Pinter is the partial delineator, rejecting naturalistic completeness of detail because such details would themselves be delusory. Thus, Boulton finds *The Caretaker* a quintessentially twentieth-century play that is also timeless in that it illustrates the dangers and desires of those who would take care.

Too specific an interpretation should be guarded against—a warning echoed by Wellwarth, who lists a good number of these interpretations in a footnote.[33] Yet perceptions can be helpful. For Wilson Knight, the room is a meaningless jumble; yet, looked at closely, the junk in the room is not without significance. Sinko sees this room as outside the normal laws of living, characterized by what he terms a particular kind of "inability." Nothing will ever get done—and this sense of inability makes the murder of Aston by Davies impossible. This surrealistic nightmare is substantiated, however, by a wealth of naturalistic detail, and Sinko is surely right in suggesting that the dialogue, moving as it does from matter-of-fact truth to lies to fantasy, blends into a harmonious whole the two sides that failed to fuse successfully in *The Birthday Party*.[34] Because of this fusion, whatever the implications of the play, *The Caretaker* remains obstinately and simply a play about two brothers and a caretaker.

CHAPTER 4

Plays for Television

W HEN Laurence Kitchin discussed the drama that he calls "compressionistic" because of its enclosed settings, limited characters, and claustrophobic atmosphere, he suggested that such drama had had its day in the live theater and that its natural home was television. The shift from theater to television, however, introduces two new problems: the medium and the audience; and the latter, at least, is remarkably difficult to evaluate. What is noteworthy is that Pinter, in writing for the apparently confined demands of television, has widened the scope of his plays. One reason for this expansion is that while the small screen seems admirably suited to a drama in one room in the way a larger theater often is not, the extreme mobility of the camera in television productions allows a greater use of sets or of half sets. The theater, which has to use the whole stage, is unable to restrict the audience's vision to one corner by use of a camera. This mobility, reflected in the plays that Pinter has written for television, anticipates the even greater mobility he enjoys in his film work.

Today, the dramatist is less than ever restricted to the theater. Indeed, economic pressures frequently drive him into the more lucrative spheres of radio, television, and cinema, where the potential audience is, of course, infinitely larger. Few contemporary dramatists have stayed in the theater. Several, including Pinter, have had experience in all four media. Moreover, Pinter's work for television seems to have helped his acceptance by audiences. Taylor is certainly justified in claiming that the general failure, both critical and commercial, of *The Birthday Party* and the triumph of *The Caretaker* were influenced by television, which, with a new production of *The Birthday Party* and *A Night Out*, introduced a large audience to Pinter's manner and themes and helped to create a climate of opinion favorable to his plays.[1] The fact that *The Caretaker* is a better play might also have had something to do with this success, but television certainly helped Pinter. Equally, working for television certainly

changed Pinter's work, or at least his work for television embodied changes in perspective in the typical Pinter play.

I *A New Kind of Play*

Leech describes Pinter's plays as taking place in a world that
is old, shabby, and sick—a Beckett-type world.[2] If this statement
were true about Pinter's work up to and including *The Caretaker* (and even there it seems more true of Beckett than of
Pinter), it no longer remains so. *A Slight Ache* proved to be the
exception; for, if translated into visual terms, the room is neither
shabby nor confined, but comfortable, even elegant, and looks
onto a large, sunny garden, a setting that is repeated in *The
Lover.* The size of Pinter's television audiences would seem to
indicate that he was watched by the masses as well as by a cul-
tured elite and that his plays can be accepted on any level as a
dramatic experience. The shabbiness of his early plays, with their
inescapable echoes of Beckett and Graham Greene (if insisted
upon), contradicts Pinter's own arguments about the meaning
of the plays; for he has been quite positive that what happens in
his plays could happen anywhere, at any time, in any place,
even though the events may seem unfamiliar at first glance. He
has also suggested that what happens in his plays is realistic but
that what he is doing is not realism.[3] This distinction is difficult
for the average audience and critic to make because realism is
overwhelmingly in the direction of a certain kind of play, and the
television audience probably is more casual in its viewing and
more conventional in its demands.

These different possibilties and demands and the audiences
make a difference that Pinter himself recognized: "I don't make
any distinction between kinds of writing, but when I write for
the stage I always keep a continuity of action. Television lends
itself to quick cutting from scene to scene, and nowadays I see
it more and more in terms of pictures. When I think of someone
knocking at a door, I see the door opening in close-up and a long
shot of someone going up the stairs. Of course the words go
with the pictures, but on television, ultimately, the words are of
less importance than they are on the stage."[4] Nor does he find
the medium confining, restrictive, or necessarily limited to
naturalistic drama. And one performance of his play on tele-

vision, *A Night Out*, had an audience of about 16 million people
—which no stage dramatist could hope for.

We are concerned in this section with the three plays Pinter
wrote *for* television, as opposed to plays that were translated
into that medium. There is a considerable and obvious difference
in the writing and the atmosphere: the wit grows more elegant,
the comedy more purely comic, and sex becomes a fully developed part of the Pinter world. In a sense, television marks
the liberation of Pinter. John Bowen, suggesting that Pinter
would some day have to burst out of his room and go down to
Sidcup, rightly thought that television might be the means of
freeing him.[5] The first actual television play, however, was something of a setback. *A Night Out*, written for radio, had been
quickly and very successfully reproduced on television in April,
1960. Soon after, on July 21st, Pinter's first play written specifically for television was produced. Called *Night School*, it was not
felt, by Pinter, to be a success. Since then, he has produced two
more plays, *The Collection* (televised in May, 1961) and *The
Lover* (televised in March, 1963), both of which have been
subsequently staged.

II Night School

Night School was felt to be a mistake, and Pinter never
published it because he thought it showed him slipping into a
formula: "Later I realised that in one short television play of
mine there were characteristics that implied I was slipping into
a formula. It so happened this was the worst thing I've written.
The words and ideas had become automatic, redundant. That
was the red light for me and I don't feel I shall fall into that pit
again."[6] But this play was seen on television; both Esslin and
Taylor appear to be familiar with it; and however bad it is, or
because of its mistakes, it is interesting. Mr. Pinter kindly sent
a copy to me with permission for quotation, and, while agreeing
with him in principle, I am inclined to think he is oversevere
and welcome its publication in 1967. Some of the verbal wit is
unfortunate, as when Solto romances about his early experiences
to the two aunts:

SOLTO: And what a trip. I was only a pubescent. I killed a man
with my own hands, a six foot ten Lascar from Madagascar.
ANNIE: From Madagascar?

[110]

SOLTO: Sure. A lascar.
ANNIE: Alaska?
SOLTO: Madagascar.

But even this cliché joke is well placed in the play and is not without its value as a cliché. Similarly, there is the familiar pun on "tart":

I bet you never had a tart in prison, Wally?
No, I couldn't lay my hands on one.

In these sections, we have part of an extensive system of food references with sexual implications used to reflect failure of communication.

Night School is chiefly remarkable, however, for the flexibility possible on television. That is to say, Pinter is able to add to the major scenes little vignettes (thus including the revue sketch material in the play) in a manner which is fully realized not in the subsequent television plays but in films like *The Servant*. The reason for the disappearance of these vignettes from the other two plays for television points up the second difference of *Night School*—the large number of major characters. In *The Collection* and in *The Lover*, Pinter returned to a limited number of characters, thus excluding fringe characters.

The play opens with Wally's return home from prison to his aunts Annie and Milly after serving nine months for forging entries in Post Office Savings Bank books. The two aunts clearly have something to tell him but are uneasy about doing it. So instead, they stuff him with food and talk about nothing. Finally, they tell him that they have let his room to a young, quiet, homely, clean girl called Sally Gibbs, a schoolteacher who goes to night school three times a week, bathes twice a day, wears a lovely perfume, and knows Wally has been in prison but not why. Wally is hurt and defensive. Although he had not contributed to the aunts' living expenses, he had bought the bed Sally is sleeping in and had been looking forward to getting back to his own room. Ironically, he complains that prison has accustomed him to privacy and that sleeping in the dining room will rob him of it. He meets Sally later when he goes up to his former room to collect some things he had left there. For her, too, the room is important—a haven, a place of peace and security. As he recovers some Post Office Bank books from a secret place in the wardrobe, he accidentally discovers a photograph of Sally that suggests that she works as a hostess in a night club. The scene fades out as Wally is starting to practise forging signatures.

The second part introduces Solto, a scrap merchant and a friend of Wally, who is having tea with the aunts and boasting about his prowess in Australia, where he discovered cricket and Bradman, and his adventures in the merchant navy. Solto cannot, however, lend Wally the £200 he asked for even if Wally is prepared to go straight and give up forgery, for which he has no talent. When Wally shows him the photograph, Solto thinks he has seen Sally somewhere and is asked by Wally to trace her. Thus, although there is every possibility that they could be friends and that Wally could regain his bed and room either by having an affair with Sally or by marrying her, he wants to know the truth. While Solto is searching, a relationship is established. As the aunts eat in bed (for them, as for Solto, food is the equivalent of sex), they hear Wally visit Sally for a cup of coffee. He takes along a bottle of brandy, and, although the photograph had shown Sally drinking, she pretends to be unused to drink. She also pretends that she is learning languages at night school and after class goes to a girl friend's flat to listen to records of Mozart and Brahms. Wally pretends that he used to plan his armed robberies in this room and that from being a successful gunman he became a successful prison librarian—so successful that he had been offered a job at the British Museum to be in charge of rare manuscripts. He also suggests that the aunts have Sally in mind as his prospective wife (the earlier discussion between Solto and the aunts was about why Wally should and did not marry), but he claims that he has been married three times already. He rapidly denies this statement, however, and makes Sally model for him. She stands up, crosses and uncrosses her legs. Finally, he kisses her. This whole scene is remarkably close to the scene between Albert and the prostitute in *A Night Out*.

Part Three begins with Solto's visit to the night club where Sally works. A scene in the dressing room shows the unsophisticated side of Sally, who is now called Katina. The camera turns to the aunts to show them rejoicing that Wally is falling for her, and the main scene shows Solto and Sally together. Solto boasts about his possessions, including a private beach. Telling her that he is looking for her, he shows her the photograph. He reveals that Wally Street, forger and petty thief, wants information about her. Esslin suggests that Solto "inadvertently" reveals this fact, but the scene strikes me as more calculated: Solto reveals this information in order to bring pressure to bear on Sally. Presumably, she complies with his wishes, since in the next scene with Walter, Solto denies finding her:

> WALTER: What's up? Have you found the girl?
> SOLTO: The girl. What girl?
> WALTER: The girl. That photo I gave you. You know.
> SOLTO: Oh the girl . . . You mean the girl I was trying to . . .
> WALTER: Yes I thought that might be why you've come around.
> SOLTO: You're dead right. That's exactly why I come round.
> WALTER: That's what I thought.
> SOLTO: And you weren't wrong.
> (*Pause.*)
> WALTER: Well. Where is she?
> SOLTO: That's what I wanted to tell you. I can't find her.
> WALTER: You can't find her!
> SOLTO: Not a smell. That's exactly what I came round to tell you.

If Solto, for whatever reason, does not want to tell, Wally by this time does not want to know and tells Solto to abandon the search. When they hear Sally coming in, Wally says it is the school-teacher, and Solto advises him to go after her because she is an educated girl. However, she will not open her door to Walter. Next morning, she leaves a note for the aunts, the Misses Billet (in the army sense of temporary lodging). So Walter gets his room back—and finds another photograph of Sally as a school-teacher with the volleyball team.

Night School was intended to be the first of a new kind of Pinter play—light comedy with new realism. Its failure stems from the fact that no author can put old wine in new bottles; it re-exploits too heavily the old themes—conflict for possession of a room (which stands for peace and security for both Wally and Sally) and lying. Wally lies to achieve his various purposes, and the contradictions tell us something about him; Solto lies, or romances, but the truth or otherwise of those stories never comes into question; Sally also lies. The question posed by the play remains: what is Sally? That question is answered by the end of the play—unless the last photograph is also phony; she is both teacher *and* night-club hostess. She is also a girl who might have helped Wally if he had not frightened her away. The problem of a girl who is both Sally and Katina is explored by Pinter later in *The Lover*.

Clearly, the play carried over too many details from *A Night Out*, but it is, in spite of bad or weak dialogue, a step forward. Not only does it rest on the dual personality of Sally, but it introduces another suggestion. In wanting his room badly, Wally loses his chance to regain it and to find a place in the world. This message seems questionable as the important one, since the play also turns crucially on identity. To impress Sally, Wally invents a character, just as she invented one to impress the aunts, and just as Solto invents one to impress Sally in the night club. No true relationship could be based on all this pretense—or could it? This question motivates the next two plays, *The Collection* and *The Lover*.

III   The Collection

The Collection was Pinter's second television play, not counting the experience gained from *A Night Out*, but it is obviously different from the earlier plays in richness of setting and of characters. In this play, the characters are not tramps but artistic men and women engaged in dress designing. A comedy of menace, the menace is so muted that it is almost not there. The action concerns two couples, James and Stella (man and wife) and Harry and Bill (whose relationship is possibly homosexual). The play describes a series of meetings between man and wife, protector and protégé, man and protégé, and protector and wife. Wellwarth, who sees the play as allusive to Genet, feels that it would be impractical for American television—a great pity, for *The Collection* is entirely suited to the medium.

The action begins with a rather sinister telephone call from James to Bill received by Harry at four o'clock in the morning. Swift scenes follow between James and Stella and Harry and Bill that illustrate the tensions and uneasiness of both relationships. After Harry has gone out, Bill receives a visit from James, who has telephoned earlier to make sure that Harry is out. James menaces Bill amiably on matters such as having no olives in the flat, but then suddenly accuses him of having slept with Stella in Leeds the week before. Bill, amused, suggests that Stella is making it up, but, when James makes a sudden aggressive movement, Bill falls to the floor. Under pressure, Bill admits that he kissed her and no more; under more pressure, he says that he did, in fact, go to bed with her.

The two short scenes that follow develop the domestic tension between the couples (that between James and Stella revolving once more around the lack of olives), and James tells Stella that Bill has confessed. She neither confirms nor denies it, but she is rather surprised that James liked Bill. James finds Bill intelligent. Bill has a collection of interesting Chinese vases, likes opera, and, in fact, reminds him of a boy at school he had liked very much. While James goes off to visit Bill again, Harry, worried by the effect James's visits are having on Bill, goes to see Stella. She tells him that James has fabricated this fantastic story after two years of happy marriage and that he has never behaved like this before, even though she is often away on business. Harry, happily reassured, admires her Persian kitten.

Meanwhile, James and Bill are getting on very well together, although the olives Bill has provided are now rejected by James. As James muses over his wife's infidelity, he plays with a cheese knife, and, as Harry enters unnoticed, James suddenly challenges Bill to a duel, throwing the knife at him. Bill clumsily catches the knife, cutting himself in the process, and Harry intervenes. Introducing himself to James,[7] he says that he has just got the whole truth from Stella: she had created the story (scarcely the story we heard!). Bill agrees, saying that he confessed only because it amused him to do so. Harry furiously explains this "amusement" in an attack on Bill:

HARRY: Bill's a slum boy, you see, he's got a slum sense of humor. That's why I never take him along with me to parties. Because he's got a slum mind. I have nothing against slum minds *per se*, you understand, nothing at all. There's a certain kind of slum mind which is perfectly all right in a slum, but when this slum mind gets out of the slum it sometimes persists, you see, it rots everything. That's what Bill is. There's something faintly putrid about him, don't you find? Like a slug. There's nothing wrong with slugs in their place, but he's a slum slug; there's nothing wrong with slum slugs in their place, but this one won't keep his place—he crawls all over the walls of nice houses, leaving slime, don't you boy? He confirms stupid little stories just to amuse himself, while everyone else has to run round in circles to get to the root of the matter and smooth the whole thing out. All he can do is sit and suck his bloody hand and decompose like the filthy putrid slum slug he is.[8]

Clearly, this humiliation of Bill by Harry tells us more about Harry than about Bill. Harry's anger and fear are those of an older man who recognizes the dangerous temptations of Stella *and* James for his younger friend. But the venom of the speech stings Bill so much that—as James and Harry are smoothing out the situation, each with the truth that satisfies him; covering up the trouble with the conventional excuse of overwork; and solving it with the conventional suggestion of a holiday abroad—he suddenly insists on telling the truth. He and Stella had just sat together downstairs and had talked about what they would do if they went up to her room. And James has to return to Stella with this story, which again she will neither confirm nor deny. The play ends on a close-up of her enigmatic smile.[9]

IV *The Implications of* The Collection

Taylor, reviewing the stage production of this play, observed that it was a comedy that started off lightly enough but turned into "something much more uncomfortable and obsessional" than the average viewer or audience expected.[10] The title presumably refers to the Chinese vases (an excellent symbol for the fragile sexual relationship, as we can see in Pope's *The Rape of the Lock*), the collection of clothes shown at Leeds, and, principally, the collection of truths the play produces. It is clearly not very important whether or not Bill and Stella *did* sleep together in Leeds; what matters is the potential that possible act contains, and the illusions to preserve or destroy it are given an extra twist because the quartet is not two men and two women, but one woman and three men. In the action, Bill and Stella (who are never allowed to meet) effectively change partners! *The Collection* is not simply a comedy of manners kept deliberately slight, as Taylor suggests. Although not a life-and-death matter, there is a question to be answered, and the reply remains teasingly out of reach. Simply, two people have to rethink their relationship in terms of two other people; and, in spite of the number of starts, of success and near-success, they fail to do so.

James's terrorization of Bill is amiable only because we know why he is doing it, but Bill initially does not. This situation is different from *The Birthday Party*, where we share the victim's terror and ignorance (or, if Stanley has ideas on the subject of his menacers, he does not share them with the audience). At the end, James is starting to question Stella again, but is getting no satisfactory answer:

The piece works, like the early plays, as a thoroughly efficient mechanism for mystifying the audience, but this time it works for their amusement rather than their terrorization. It is an elaborate game, by the rules of which, clearly, we are permitted practically every possible combination of the principals except that of the two people Bill and Stella, who were actually present on the occasion in question (if they *were* there, of course), and who alone could perhaps tell us what really happened. For the moment the piece represents Pinter's last word on the subjects of menace and verification, two obsessive preoccupations of his early work, and it cannot be entirely coincidental that he has his say completely in terms of comedy.[11]

What has happened in the play is that two relationships that had rather fallen into habit have been jolted, and the two people in each have had to rethink the basis for their relationships. This rethinking is reflected in small details, such as James's demand for olives (which he does not like) and in Bill's declining potatoes with the Sunday roast (which he has always had). The wisdom of hindsight suggests that this comedy did not entirely lack sinister implications. The permutations remind us of Iris Murdoch's *A Severed Head*, and the homosexuality, particularly felt in *The Dwarfs*, is now more explicit. At any rate, sex is part of the Pinter world; in the next comedy, *The Lover*, it is combined with wit. After *The Lover*, Taylor revised the passage cited above as follows:

The business of verification, of finding out "the truth," has become an elaborate maneouvre, a highly serious game like something in *Les Liaisons Dangereuses* (here, for instance, every possible combination of the principals is permitted except that of the two people, Bill and Stella who were actually present on the occasion in question—if they *were* there, of course—and who alone could perhaps tell us what really happened), but in which what is to be decided may well be a matter of life and death. It is vitally important to James that he should find out what sort of woman Stella is, faced suddenly with a picture of an unknown woman who yet lies in the same body with his wife. Which is the real Stella? If he knows the "facts" for certain, will he be any nearer a solution? Can the game be played through to a decisive conclusion, or is it doomed to end in deadlock?[12]

Taylor's is an *ex post facto* interpretation in the light of *The Lover* that takes James's predicament over Stella as its subject. It is surely no accident that in the first interview between James and Bill, the word "wife" is conjoined with the word "whore," a conjunction central to the last play. But the clue appeared earlier in the character of Sally-Katina in *Night School*.

Pinter, having taken us into the more terrifying corners of the human condition, now begins to use menace and lies as part of the fabric of life in order to build up what he has disintegrated. He produces a play that is nearer Pirandello's comic vein than Beckett's dark comedy, but Pinter is still concerned with the ambiguities of truth: "Against the background of a very ordinary bedroom farce, Pinter traces this very extraordinary story of an attempt to get at truth; it is not that the people involved are trying to conceal their misdemeanours, or develop their fantasies, by means of lying, for the confusion lies deeper than that. Each one is deliberately withdrawn, not only from contact with the other—though this also enters into it through the desultory but real conversation, not the stylized fantasy of Ionesco—but from fitting himself into a pattern of real events."[13] The strange menage of *The Lover* represents a kind of answer to James's problem in *The Collection*, where the question is not likely to bring James satisfaction because he is naïve enough to insist on truth. The motive lies in his remark to Bill: "When you treat my wife like a whore then I'm entitled to know what you've got to say about it."

V   The Lover

The Lover, which Wellwarth regards as one of the most brilliant plays in the English language since the war, was essentially for television. The influence of the medium is demonstrated by the opening shots of bongo drums (an echo of Stanley's drum in *The Birthday Party*?), a close-up lost in a stage production. The play is, in fact, full of details that show Pinter's absorption with technique, and the stage directions, which have always been explicit and lengthy, now contain phrases like "cut" and "shot" and other purely televisional instructions.

The setting of the play is spacious and luxurious—a house in the country, near Windsor, in the summer—and is in sharp contrast to the earlier rooms in a town in winter. The story, too is opposite; illusion—previously used as escape, withdrawal, or betrayal—now preserves a marriage partly based on the French recipe that every wife should also be a mistress. The opening of the play is witty and startling:

RICHARD (*amiably*): Is your lover coming today?
SARAH: Mmnn.
RICHARD: What time?
SARAH: Three.
RICHARD: Will you be going out . . . or staying in?
SARAH: Oh . . . I think we'll stay in.
RICHARD: I thought you wanted to go to that exhibition?
SARAH: I did, yes . . . but I think I'd prefer to stay in with him today.
RICHARD: Mmn-hmmn. Well, I must be off.
SARAH: Mmnnn.
RICHARD: Will he be staying long do you think?
SARAH: Mmmnnn. . . .
RICHARD: About . . . six, then?
SARAH: Yes.
RICHARD: Have a pleasant afternoon.
SARAH: Mmnn.
RICHARD: Bye-bye.
SARAH: Bye.

Sarah, who changes into high heels and a tight, black, "sexy dress," settles down to wait for her lover. The doorbell rings, and, as she opens the door to him, the scene fades. Richard returns in the early evening, and after he poses polite questions about her afternoon and whether or not it was pleasant, he startles her by asking if she ever thinks of him working hard at the office while she is being unfaithful to him at home. She replies that at certain moments she does think of him, but the picture is not terribly convincing. After changing her shoes (she has forgotten to remove the high-heeled afternoon shoes), she tells him why. She says that he is not working hard at the office; he is spending the afternoon with his mistress. Richard admits to a whore, but not to a mistress—and to a whore, moreover, who lacks the grace, elegance, and wit that Sarah expects:

RICHARD (*laughing*): These terms just don't apply. You can't sensibly enquire whether a whore is witty. It's of no significance whether she is or she isn't. She's simply a whore, a functionary who either pleases or displeases.

SARAH: And she pleases you?

RICHARD: Today she is pleasing. Tomorrow . . . ? One can't say.

(*Pause.*)

SARAH: I must say I find your attitude to women rather alarming.

RICHARD: Why? I wasn't looking for a woman I could respect, as you, whom I could admire and love, as I do you. Was I? All I wanted was . . . how shall I put it . . . someone who could express and engender lust with all lust's cunning. Nothing more.[14]

This amusing, heartless dialogue, reminiscent of Restoration comedy, becomes serious only in the light of the information given us at the end of the act. His asking questions about what Sarah does in the afternoon is, apparently, not in the rules of the game and upsets Sarah. She is reassured, however, that things are "beautifully balanced." She prepares for another afternoon.

At this point Pinter introduces a third character. When the doorbell rings, Sarah opens it, and the milkman, John, offers (with whatever symbolism the attentive reader may supply) her cream. Sarah declines. The next ring announces her lover, and the door opens to reveal Richard dressed casually in light slacks and a suede jacket. Sarah calls him Max.

Act Two concerns the games Max-Richard and Sarah play in the afternoon. Once more the camera shows passionate tapping on the bongo drums, and then the two begin to play their parts. First, Max is a lecherous stranger making advances to an unwilling Sarah; then Max is a kind park-keeper who rescues Sarah and then has to fight off her sexual advances until they both fall to the floor in the tea-time game. These games, clearly defined by custom, are also threatened by Max-Richard, who once more starts to ask questions. Max asks where her husband is and says that he must give her up because his wife does not know what he is doing:

MAX: No, she doesn't know. She thinks I know a whore, that's all. Some spare-time whore, that's all. That's what she thinks.
SARAH: Yes, but be sensible . . . my love . . . she doesn't mind, does she?
MAX: She'd mind if she knew the truth, wouldn't she?
SARAH: What truth? What are you talking about?
MAX: She'd mind if she knew that, in fact . . . I've got a full-time mistress, two or three times a week, a woman of grace, elegance, wit, imagination—
SARAH: Yes, yes, you have—
MAX: In an affair that's been going on for years.[15]

This line of argument from Max naturally surprises Sarah. Max, he says, has played his last game; he must think of his wife and of the children who will soon be home from boarding school. And when Sarah tries to play the "tea-time" game to distract him, he quite coolly rejects her because she is too bony:

MAX: You're not plump enough. You're nowhere near plump enough. You know what I like. I like enormous women. Like bullocks with udders. Vast great uddered bullocks.
SARAH: You mean cows.
MAX: I don't mean cows. I mean voluminous great uddered feminine bullocks. Once, years ago, you vaguely resembled one.
SARAH: Oh, thanks.
MAX: But now, quite honestly, compared to my ideal . . . you're skin and bone.
They stare at each other.
He puts on his jacket.
SARAH: You're having a lovely joke.
MAX: It's no joke.
He goes.[16]

When Richard returns from a tiring day at the office, he finds that Sarah's afternoon has not been a success. He is fairly sympathetic, but he objects to a cold dinner, suggesting tartly that Sarah's afternoon pastimes are beginning to interfere with her wifely duties. In answer to Sarah's question about his whore's being bony he replies confusingly that he likes thin women! Richard now begins a new game, namely, to forbid Max entry to the house—Sarah may no longer receive him there. He "discovers" the bongo drums and asks what their purpose is, upsetting Sarah, who points out that the arrangement was simply: no questions asked. When Richard perseveres, she retaliates:

You paltry, stupid . . . ! Do you think he's the only one who comes! Do you? Do you think he's the only one I entertain? Mmmnnn? Don't be silly. I have other visitors, other visitors, all the time, I receive all the time. Other afternoons, all the time. When neither of you know, neither of you. I give them strawberries in season. With cream. Strangers, total strangers. But not to me, not while they're here. They come to see the hollyhocks. And then they stay for tea. Always. Always.[17]

The scene with John, the milkman, in Act One suggests that this assertion is probably not true, but Richard-Max cannot be sure. At any rate, he stops his new little game and moves back into the park game. Gradually, although dressed for the evening, the two slip into the sequence of characters they assume every afternoon until Richard tells Sarah to change her clothes and calls her his lovely whore.

VI   *The Meaning of* The Lover

There is an obvious streak of sado-masochism in the games played in *The Lover*, but it should not be accounted as too unusual. As Anthony Storr points out in his recent book, *Sexual Deviations*:

It is only when sado-masochism is extreme or divorced from sexual intercourse that it can be counted a deviation. For countless couples engage in minor sado-masochistic rituals which serve the purpose of arousing them erotically, and are thus valuable introductory steps to the sexual act itself. Are there any two lovers who have not played some version of the age-old game in which one dominates and the other submits, or who have not teasingly tormented each other by pretending to kiss and then withdrawing? Such games may seem remote from the floggings of a de Sade or the humiliation of a Sacher-Masoch, but both spring from the same fundamental roots.[18]

The games in the play are elaborate and ritualistic; not only do they separate the respectable husband-wife relationship from the more passionate lover-mistress relationship (with a yet finer distinction between mistress and whore), but even within the lover-mistress relationship the positions change rapidly from domination to dominated, from modesty to shameless immodesty.[19] The separation of roles seems to have become so complete that Sarah and Richard begin to act as though they were being unfaithful; they even become jealous of their alter egos! The play that most immediately invites comparison is Osborne's *Under Plain Cover* (the second of the *Plays for England*), but Pinter's treatment, as Taylor points out, is deeper: "It is not just a game for keeping marriage fresh and exciting, but an acceptance of the inescapable fact that each person is 'the sum of so many reflections.' . . . And it all amounts to a successfully working marriage of ten years' standing, with children (at boarding school) and no outside involvements."[20] But I wonder if we can believe in the children? Osborne's husband and wife have two babies who are actually brought on stage. The Osborne play is less concerned with the games played by the young (and unfortunately incestuous) couple than with a personal diatribe on press intrusion in the name of public service. *Under Plain Cover* becomes only a cheaply sensational story of the kind it purports to be protesting against. The incest is an extra twist necessary for the major theme, since the games played privately would not constitute a reason for press intrusion. The games in *Under Plain Cover* are also more physically perverse, involving, as the title implies, a great deal of equipment of a fetishistic nature. In *The Lover*, actual "equipment" is kept minimal; if we take the children seriously (and ten years), then, as with James and Stella after two years, the time has come to take stock of the situation—in Richard's and Sarah's case, to connect the afternoon with the evening—to get Max to dinner. Taylor sums up the situation in the play as follows:

Any menace to the *status quo* comes from within; if the arrangement looks like breaking down, it is only because the desire to have things clear and unequivocal is part of basic human nature and almost impossible to vanquish. However Richard and Sarah appreciate the necessity of vanquishing it, the impossibility indeed of living together on any other terms except the acceptance of an infinitude of reflections in lieu of the unknowable, perhaps non-existent essence. So perhaps if Max, Richard's lover-persona, can visit in the evening as well as the afternoon. . . .[21]

But we must distinguish between the need for clarification and what needs to be clarified. The questions asked by Richard (like the questions asked by the husband in Albee's *Who's Afraid of Virginia Woolf*) are aimed—almost maliciously it seems in both cases, and in Richard's case for no obvious reason—not so much at destroying illusions as incorporating them into reality: doing away with the fancy clothes and the stage props and incorporating the passion of the afternoon in the husband-wife relationship. Richard's demand for a feminine bullock seems to suggest that Sarah's urges must be as strong as his and unhampered by her status as woman and wife.

VII   *Criticism of* The Lover

The critics who saw Pinter's recent stage production of this essay in verification (in a double bill with *The Dwarfs*, which perhaps explains why Taylor, above, explains it in terms of that play) seemed baffled, in spite of the fact that it was not a new play to them. It remained for the reviewer of *The Financial Times* to treat the play seriously and to see the obvious affinity with Osborne's *Under Plain Cover*. He pointed out that the elegance and wit were important, conferring upon the situation what Osborne could not: "For, where Mr. Osborne is a moralist who must give rein to his indignation, Mr. Pinter is an analyst and stylist. Mr. Osborne rails at life, Mr. Pinter notes its patterns and arranges it." Harold Hobson, in *The Sunday Times*, cited the medieval *cours d'amour*, where it was publically debated which of the two was the better—husband or lover; but only Bamber Gascoigne, in *The Observer*, looked at the structure of the play. He noticed a shift in the play, pointing out that Act Two destroys (I would suggest "qualifies") what has gone before, making two plays, of which the second gradually develops into a new theme on a different level: "It now becomes an expressionistic drama about a young couple who can't reconcile their respectable idea of marriage with the violent ritual of their sexual passions. So they keep sex in a separate compartment, until at last the husband dares to introduce the ritual into their starchy evening life—to the terror, at first, of the wife, but then to her gradual and mounting delight." And, we might add, to ours. For with this play, Pinter opened up a very promising new kind of drama that he has yet to develop further.

CHAPTER 5

Interim Reports

BETWEEN 1960 AND 1965, Pinter was not too productive, although it must be remembered that the plays produced so
rapidly had been written over a longer period of time. Including
the rejected play *Night School*, he wrote only three short plays
for television; three or four more sketches, including a special
cricket sketch performed by Pinter and Pleasance at a charity
show given by the Lord Taverners; and a short story. The new
sketches, presented by Michael Bakewell on the British Broadcasting Corporation "Third Program," consisted of "Applicant,"
already published; "Dialogue for Three," published in *Stand*
magazine; and three that have not yet been published—"That's
All," "That's Your Trouble," and "Interview"—all slight examples
of Pinter's comedy. In "That's All," Mrs. A and Mrs. B discuss the
day on which they and a third woman visit the butcher and afterwards make a cup of tea; in "That's Your Trouble," two men-
about-town discuss in a park the strains imposed upon a man
who is carrying a sandwich-board; and in "Interview," Mr.
Jakes (i.e., a privy) is interviewed about trade in his pornograph-
ic book shop. As Bakewell commented in *The Radio Times*, the
sketches show Pinter working in miniature "with all his remarkable feeling for the subtleties, manners and banalities of speech
and action."

I *"Tea Party"*

The short story "Tea Party," also broadcast in 1964, was read
by Pinter himself on the "Third Program" and later published
in *Playboy* magazine. The story is about a man whose suspicions
of those about him—his wife, sons, brother-in-law, and secretary
—induce periods of blindness during which, as he loses his grip
on reality, he finds his skills and abilities being slowly destroyed.
In its use of blindness, various kinds of weather, and the loss of
skills, this story is strongly reminiscent of *A Slight Ache*.

A man—with a wife, two sons, a brother-in-law as business partner, and a perfect secretary—who has been very successful at business, in making love, at carpentry, and at ping-pong, is waiting for his physician to remove the bandages from his eyes. As he reflects on his relationships with these people, and on his failing abilities, he feels that all of his friends and relations are cheating him and that his wife is being seduced. But he concludes that these events could not surely be happening at a tea party with all his family present. The story provides an interesting comparison with *A Slight Ache* (where Edward had been a failure, probably for financial as well as sexual reasons) because the protagonist's insecurity seems to stem from his success.

II *Pinter's Work for the Cinema*

Pinter was, of course, extremely busy in the new medium of the cinema, where he was a close collaborator in two films— author of both scripts, associate producer in one, and actor in the other. Besides the film of *The Caretaker*, there was *The Servant*. Pinter also wrote the script for the film version of Penelope Mortimer's novel *The Pumpkin Eater* and a screenplay, as yet unfilmed, called *The Compartment*. He has just (1967) finished the scripts for two films, *The Quiller Memorandum*, filmed by Ivan Foxwell and directed by Michael Anderson, and *Accident* directed by Joseph Losey and starring, once more, Dirk Bogarde. *The Quiller Memorandum*, adapted by Pinter from Adam Hall's spy-thriller, with George Segal as Quiller, received a mixed press when it was released in November, 1966, but critics were unanimous in their praise of *Accident* when it was released in February, 1967. *Accident*, an adaptation of Nicholas Mosley's stream-of-consciousness novel, was described by Penelope Houston in *Spectator* (February 17, 1967) as a "compellingly articulate movie" and both Penelope Gilliat in *The Observer* (February 12, 1967) and Dilys Powell in *The Sunday Times* (February 12, 1967) supported this view. In an interview about the film written by John Russell Taylor in *Sight and Sound* (Autumn, 1966) Pinter reiterated his views on drama and mystery:

I do so hate the becauses of drama. Who are we to say that this happens because that happened, that one thing is the consequence of another? How do we know? What reason have we to suppose that life is so neat and tidy? The most we know for sure is that the things which have happened have happened in a certain order: any connections we think we see, or choose to make, are pure guesswork. Life is much more mysterious than plays make it out to be. And it is this mystery which fascinates me: what happens between the words, what happens when no words are spoken. . . . In this film everything happens, nothing is explained. It has been pared down and down, all unnecessary words and actions are eliminated. If it is interesting to see a man cross a room, then we see him do it; if not, then we leave out the insignificant stages of the action. I think you'll be surprised at the directness, the simplicity with which Losey is directing this film: no elaborations, no odd angles, no darting about. Just a level, intense look at people, at things. As though if you look at them hard enough they will give up their secrets. Not that they will, for however much you see and guess at there is always that something more. . . .

Success certainly seems to have distracted Pinter from the medium of the theater, but the vital question is whether or not working for the cinema has spoiled him as a dramatist.

The film of *The Caretaker*, discussed in Chapter 3, is a masterpiece. *The Servant*, directed by Joseph Losey (who had had to leave Hollywood for Europe by 1953 because of the effects of McCarthyism), has been very successful: Dirk Bogarde in the leading role was partly responsible for this. Pinter had already written a version of *The Servant* (adapted from the short novel of that name by Robin Maugham) for Michael Anderson before he worked on *The Caretaker*. But when Losey decided to produce the film, Pinter largely rewrote this version for him. In dealing with a film, the literary critic is at a considerable disadvantage, since the evidence is transitory. No text properly exists of a film (although Mr. Losey kindly made available a copy of the release script, from which the quotations are taken). Moreover, the writer, more than ever part of a team, is very much at the mercy of director, cameramen, and box office. Pinter has been remarkably fortunate in his films in working with a team that has permitted both *The Servant* and *The Pumpkin Eater* to be Pinteresque films even when the script is not particularly typical Pinter dialogue. Maugham's story itself was a little Pinteresque, and Losey's work, with its characteristic cages and its destruction of the individual as leitmotifs,[1] was congenial to Pinter.

When asked about changes, Pinter replied: "Well I don't know exactly. I followed it up. I think I did change it in a number of ways. I cut out the particular, a narrator in fact, which I didn't think was very valuable to a film, but I think I did change it quite a lot in one way or another, but I kept to the main core at the same time the end is not quite the same ending that it was in the book. I must have *carte blanche* you know, to explore it."[2] The elimination of Maugham's tedious narrator is certainly the most important change, for Richard Merton (as he is called) in his relationship with Tony is the oddest thing in the book. But Pinter has also eliminated some of the preciseness of Tony's background: he left Cambridge where he was reading law to join the army in 1939; since his parents were dead and since he was unmarried, the army took the place of a family in his life. At the beginning of the novel, Tony has presumably been demobilized after five years in the Orient and is preparing to study law again. He introduces Merton to Sally Grant, his girl friend, who works in the Foreign Office and whose parents were friends of his parents. References to the "black market" locate the time of the novel fairly accurately as immediately postwar. Tony moves into a furnished apartment with the new servant, Barrett, whom Merton finds repellent (he is described as a baroque angel stuck on a gothic spire!). But Barrett is perfect for Tony, who says of him: "He insulates me from a cold drab world."[3]

Although Sally is very much in love with Tony, they have never been lovers, and she is worried about Barrett's influence. Merton assures her that Tony is perfectly normal in his sexual habits, but he also grows worried. Tony refuses to get rid of Barrett, who is, after all perfect for him, even if it means taking on Barrett's niece as maid. This niece, a girl of about sixteen, is introduced into the furnished apartment. Merton grows more and more alarmed at the insulation and even tentatively suggests to Tony that he should get out and enjoy things of the flesh, if not of the spirit. Tony cheerfully replies on the subject of sex: "No, he [Barrett] doesn't provide that. Though I daresay he would if I gave him half a chance. But I don't need sex all that much, I'd far rather have a good meal and go to bed early."[4]

Immediately after this statement, however, he goes to bed with Barrett's niece, Vera. This betrayal of his perfect servant makes Tony irritable, just as his passion for Vera further insulates him from the world of work, law, Sally, and his friends. He goes for a holiday to visit an aunt in Cornwall (Vera has had to go home to Manchester for her holiday), and during his absence, Merton, passing the house, sees a light burning in Tony's room. Thinking that Tony has returned unexpectedly, Merton lets himself in and finds Hugo Barrett and Vera together in Tony's bed. When Tony learns of this and confronts them, Barrett, who reveals that Vera is really his fiancée, suggests that servant and master are more or less in the same position. Tony throws them out and goes to stay with Merton. After a night out with an anonymous woman, he, disgusted with himself, goes down to Cornwall again.

When he returns fresh and healthy, he resumes his old life with Sally until he meets Barrett in a pub and takes him back. Sally marries another man and leaves for Rhodesia, while Tony settles down again to the comfort that Barrett alone can provide for him. Merton recognizes defeat, for Barrett has, in fact, replaced the only woman who really loved Tony—his Nanny. When Merton meets Vera, now a prostitute, he learns that Barrett knew all the time about her and Tony. She becomes nasty when Merton refuses to sleep with her. Merton rushes off to tell Tony that Vera is now a prostitute, but Barrett's hold is complete. The arrival of a very young girl to amuse Tony and Barrett and Tony's refusal of help from Merton end the novel in cold darkness.

The two main problems of the film based on *The Servant* were the heroine, Susan, and the latent homosexuality that carried over from the novel in spite of the suppression of the old-maidish narrator. Susan's background in the film was extremely vague, indeed weak, as Losey admits:

The character of the girl, the fiancée, was also intended, once Wendy Craig was cast, to be played as "posh." . . . The character of the fiancée could have come from a recently moneyed family. Her education was good, her mind better than that of Tony, but she still suffers from the terrible handicaps and social disadvantages of anyone slightly lower in the scale of the British class system. When she acts as upper-class "bitch," she is trying to do something which is neither possible for her from the point of view of character, nor her class background. I am afraid I failed to make this clear and so did the script.[5]

Susan, a very minor character in the original novel, was not, apparently, very much more in the original screenplay. But the elimination of the narrator (the antagonist in the novel) clearly required the substitution of a more strongly defined fiancée to cover episodes that were the narrator's. In the film, Susan and Tony discover Barrett in bed with Vera (poignantly, when they themselves are just about to get into it together); and it is Susan who goes to Tony at the end of the film to plead with him and is defeated by Barrett. Similarly, there is a certain symbolic significance in changing Tony from a lawyer to an architect whose father has just died, leaving him vaguely wealthy, thus freeing him to return from working somewhere in Africa. He has projects for building great cities in Brazil, but produces only dreams and a stunted obelisk and is gradually reduced to crossword puzzles (a hint from the novel that is intensified).

It is, of course, interesting to see how hints from the novel are picked up and used by Pinter. Thus, the simple line "Barrett's mulled some claret" becomes a weak joke on Claretty Barrett[6] that introduces the nickname from the army, Basher Barrett (because he was a good driller). The significant comment on the nanny introduced toward the end of the novel appears early in the film when Barrett is steeping Tony's feet in hot water after he has caught a cold and when Tony says that Barrett is too skinny to be a Nanny.[7] The dripping tap casually mentioned in Maugham[8] becomes a visual accompaniment to Tony's seduction of Vera (if that is the right word for it), an image carried over with its sexual implications into the shower game. The casually mentioned meeting with Barrett in the pub is decorated in the film with a splendidly Pinteresque character in a confidential monologue that, with its visual inconsequence, enriches the film:

MAN: I had a bit of bad luck today. . . . I really had a bit of bad luck. . . . It'll take me a few days to get over it, I can tell you. . . . Eh? . . . You're right there. *He downs beer and exits.*[9]

Even the simple line in the novel that Vera has run off with a bookie is made more precise and comical by locating the anonymous bookie in Wandsworth.

Since the struggle in the film is between Barrett and the fiancée, Pinter has been able to add scenes in which Merton could not participate. Thus, as suggested above, part of the horror of the discovery of Barrett and Vera together in Tony's bed is that Tony and Susan have just decided to use it themselves, and part of Tony's weakness of character is illustrated by the fact that after the discovery, he still wants to do so. Pinter also adds the little games played out between Tony and Barrett—the ball game on the stairs, and a sinister game of hide-and-seek in the shower (apparently a private joke about the film *Psycho*)— to emphasize the gradual degradation of Tony. And the final party *is* a party, not just one very young girl. This party, which first attracted Losey to the script, was intended to balance the homosexual tendencies in the film. At it, Susan makes a final effort to save Tony by kissing Barrett. However, Tony is incapable physically, let alone morally, of doing anything, and she stumbles out into the darkness, leaving him to his elected fate.

The crux of the film is clearly: what is it supposed to mean? That meaning is inevitably concerned with the latent homosexual elements in the film. Losey, in his interview on the subject, said that the film was really about servility: ". . . the extraordinary pervasive servility which is so evident everywhere today. People are afraid of money, of their bosses, their teachers, their wives. They are loaded with guilt by their religious and social codes— it is about the servility both of the servants and the masters. It is a product of the general corruption amidst which we live, the kind of hypocrisy common to all of us."[10]

Both Losey and Pinter regarded the servant as a victim and as "sympathetic," and Losey feels that his remark about the film— that it was the story of a Faust—has obscured this interpretation. The relationship between Barrett and Tony is treated naturally on two levels—the sociological and the sexual—and Losey insists that the homosexuality is only latent, that the final party was included to prevent a purely homosexual conclusion being drawn. However, it is difficult to imagine the person envisaged by Losey who will not see this element at all. The games played around the house are far from innocent, the memories hark back to army days, and the kind of women used are all part of the corruption of an indolent young man who sells his soul and birthright not to the devil but for one of Barrett's much-praised soufflés. But the evidence is more inconclusive in the film than in the novel; in the novel, both ladies, who should know, find Tony and Barrett odd.[11]

III *Pinter's Additions*

Pinter has also been able to add scenes, sketches integrated into the basic plot line that throw up correlative failures and perversions in the gloomy snow-and-rain world of the film. For example, there is a nasty scene when Barrett is telephoning Bolton for his "sister" Vera, and the telephone box is surrounded by young, short-skirted girls who want to get into the box out of the cold. There are two short scenes in the country at the Mountsets, a scene in a restaurant, and a short episode at Nick's Diner. Both the restaurant and the Mountset scenes give Pinter opportunities for comic sketches that reveal his continuing flair for treating noncommunication and sinister suggestion. Three episodes illustrate this quality. The first two, from the restaurant scene, provide a background for lunch with Tony and Susan. The third is from the first visit to the country:

> GIRL: He's a wonderful wit.
> MAN: Terribly funny.
> DEB.: Terribly.
> MAN: Cheers.
> DEB.: Cheers. . . . I'm dying to see him again. I haven't seen him for ages.
> MAN: You won't for some time.
> DEB.: Oh—why?
> MAN: He's in prison.[12]

Later:

> DEB.: They were gorgeous—absolutely gorgeous.
> MAN: Were they really?
> DEB.: Divine darling, but I simply couldn't get them on.
> MAN: A pity.[13]

Then there is the enigmatic conversation between two women:

> OLDER WOMAN: What did she say to you?
> YOUNGER WOMAN: Nothing.

OLDER WOMAN: Oh yes she did. She said something to you.

YOUNGER WOMAN: She didn't. She didn't really.

OLDER WOMAN: She did. I saw her mouth move . . . she whispered something to you . . . she whispered something to you, didn't she? What was it? What did she whisper to you?

YOUNGER WOMAN: She didn't whisper anything to me. She didn't whisper anything.[14]

In context, these cameos are remarkable for their suggestiveness. Much less sinister is the discussion in the country about Brazil between Tony, Susan, and the Mountsets:

LADY M.: That's where the Ponchos are, of course—on the plains.

SUSAN: Ponchos?

LORD M.: South American cowboys.

SUSAN: Are they called Ponchos?

LORD M.: They were in my day.

SUSAN: Aren't they those things they wear . . . you know with the hole in the middle for the head to go through?

LORD M.: What do you mean?

SUSAN: Well you know . . . hanging down in front and behind the cowboy.

LADY M.: They're called cloaks dear.[15]

Pinter was awarded the British Screenwriters Guild Annual Award in 1964 for the best dramatic screenplay for his work in *The Servant*, and critics have on the whole been impressed by the film. Many have remarked about its wit, and some of them, like Penelope Gilliatt, *The Observer* (November 17, 1963) have also noted that the typical room of the early Pinter play has now widened into a malignant house, an idea fruitfully explored by Taylor: "Tony's house is a sophisticated upper-class extension of the recurrent symbol in Pinter's early plays, the room-womb which offers a measure of security in an insecure world, an area of light in the surrounding darkness. But here the security is a trap sprung on the occupant by his own promptings and by the servant who embodies them and knows too well how to exploit them."[16]

IV   The Pumpkin Eater

Pinter also wrote the screenplay for *The Pumpkin Eater*, produced by Jack Clayton, whose *Room at the Top* (1958) pioneered a movement in British films. *The Pumpkin Eater* (the title is taken from the nursery rhyme about Peter the Pumpkin Eater who had a wife and could not keep her, so he put her in a pumpkin shell, and there he kept her very well), the film of Penelope Mortimer's novel, was an unusual choice for Pinter. The novel tells intimately, and from the wife's point of view, the story of a clash between two urges—that of a husband to escape from the children by working and having affairs with other women and that of the wife to go on having children. There also seems to be the usual twentieth-century implication that success in material things spoils life. At the beginning of the novel, the heroine, beautifully portrayed by Anne Bancroft, who has had several husbands and a large number of children, is having some kind of nervous breakdown. She traps her husband into giving her a child and then is herself trapped into having an hysterectomy. At the end of the novel, she is reconciled with her husband and children in a large, new house built on a hill in the country. Such a story, told entirely from the wife's point of view with no means of satisfying ourselves that she is a reliable narrator, presented a situation that I found incomprehensible—and not even the wry tone of telling made the heroine particularly interesting. Perhaps this explains why the subject seems so unusual for Pinter.

For, except in *The Lover* (and even there the dialogue is mainly from the husband-lover angle), Pinter has not relied on women for his main character. In *The Pumpkin Eater* she *is* the story. The film treats the subject very objectively, which to a certain extent counteracts the possible difficulty of making a woman the central character but, at the same time, seems to prevent understanding even more why Mrs. Jake Armitage is as she is. Unfortunately, no release script is available, but the dialogue in the film does not seem remarkably important. It is the camera work that produces the objective, elegant treatment characteristic of the film.

The *Sunday Times* (Color Supplement, April 26, 1964), remarking that the script was remarkably faithful to the novel, felt that the dialogue showed Pinter's "mastery of the casually overheard remark, significant in its sinister ambiguity" and that it was admirably suited to the depiction of a "nervous breakdown against a background of meaningless social activity." In fact, the personal tone of the novel is lost in the film. Although Pinter is able to introduce sketches that take place in a beauty parlor and at a typical Pinter party, the actual breakdown, which occurs in a leading London store, is done visually, not verbally. It is difficult to say how much of this visual work is inspired by Pinter's script—particularly in the light of his next film script, where the visual elements are prescribed, as they may very well have been in *The Pumpkin Eater*.

The critics also shared the view that Pinter and the novel were inappropriate companions. Ian Wright in *The Guardian* (July 17, 1964) felt that both Clayton and Pinter had tried to do too much justice to the novel: "Pinter's script too often becomes what it should never be—stagey. His dialogue, accurate and deadly, does not need the dramatic pointing it is so often given here." David Robinson in *The Financial Times* (July 17, 1964) concentrated on the difficulty mentioned above, namely, that there is tension between the objectivity of the camerawork and the subjectivity of the actress playing the leading role. One consequence of this division is that the actress appears more interesting and attractive than the role she plays. In *The Observer* (July 19, 1964) Penelope Gilliatt felt that Pinter, because he was such a remarkable writer with an achieved dramatic style, pushed this battle between subjectivity and objectivity his own way and that we simply do not know enough about the central character to prevent the film from seeming a shade mechanical. Dilys Powell, *The Sunday Times* (July 19, 1964) reached a conclusion directly opposed to this one, praised the film for its elegance of style but felt that it was really Clayton's film, not Pinter's. In short, the film was well received but not with unqualified enthusiasm.

V   The Compartment

The unfilmed script, *The Compartment*, is, however, much more in keeping with Pinter's subject and manner. This scenario also illustrates how completely Pinter seems to have mastered the art of using visual rather than verbal images in the cinema. The fact that *The Compartment* was to form part of a trilogy with short films by Beckett and Ionesco may have suggested some of the treatment to Pinter, for the script certainly reads as one of Pinter's most symbolic works. Perhaps symbolic is a misleading term. The constant alternation of summer and winter, day and night, hot and cold may very well simply indicate only the passage of time; but the alternating at least serves to remind us of earlier uses of weather that were not without emblematic significance.

The subject of *The Compartment* is, once more, three people and a room. Much of the action of the film, as indicated in the script, is visual, so that none of the dialogue is separate enough or indeed significant enough for quotation by itself. The film opens outside in the dark on a wet winter's night. Stott, in a raincoat, and Jane are looking at the light shining out from a basement flat. Inside in the light, in a warm and comfortable room, Tim Law is sitting by the fire and reading. When the bell rings, he answers it, greets Stott affectionately, taking off his coat, producing a towel and slippers, and offers a drink, or coffee, and a bed for the night. His hospitality is only partly checked when Stott says he has a friend with him and asks if she may come in too. Jane enters, and as Stott starts putting out the lights, she climbs into bed, where Stott joins her. Tim settles down by the one shaded lamp, and while Stott and Jane make love, continues to read his illustrated edition of a Persian love manual. Apparently, Tim has shared a flat previously with Stott and remembers the relationship with pleasure. Although his present flat is more comfortable, and although he insists that he is happy, he confesses that he sometimes gets lonely living alone.

The film shifts to the beach on a summer's day. Jane is making sand castles, and Tim is talking about Stott who is, according to Tim, a brilliant Sanskrit scholar and connected with the French aristocracy. At night, after Stott and Jane have made love, she leans over and smiles at Tim.

Stott begins to change the room, first removing the pictures and finally replacing the furniture with modern Scandinavian furniture—only the bed and the curtains remain the same. With Jane as a spectator, Stott and Tim run a race, but, when Stott does not run, Tim looks back and falls. At this point, Tim suggests that three in one room are a bit of a crowd. However, Stott is perfectly happy. In the next scene on the beach, Jane is trying to get rid of Stott so that she and Tim can live comfortably together, but Tim tells Stott of Jane's intention and protests that she is dirtying his clean Scandinavian furniture. Stott apparently falls ill and nearly dies, but he convalesces in a room now decorated in the grand Italian manner, with Tim playing a flute. Throwing marbles at him, Stott hits him in the face, and after Tim has shattered a golden fish tank with a marble, Stott knocks him down with a marble aimed at his head.

While Jane is making instant coffee in the kitchen, Stott and Tim, in a now completely bare room, advance on each other, each with a broken milk bottle in the hand. They parry and smash together. The camera moves to the first shot of a cold, dark, wet exterior where Tim, wearing Stott's raincoat, and Jane, huddled once more under the wall, are looking at light coming from the basement flat. Inside, the room is furnished as it was at the beginning, and Stott is reading comfortably by the fire. When the bell rings, he opens the door and greets Tim enthusiastically. The question remains as to whether or not Stott will invite Jane in and begin the action again.

The furnishing of the room, the possession of the room, the sex, and the little games played between the men show a distinct affinity with the material in *The Servant*, and neither that film nor *The Compartment* is really alien to the Pinter of the theater. Some sort of strong relationship between the two men survives in which girl and room become a kind of battleground. This battle seems to be the action of the play. Its meaning, the film itself may resolve. One notices that in the second transformation of the room, the bed has disappeared; by the third, all the furniture has disappeared. After the fight, when Stott and Tim have changed places, the original furniture is back. It also remains to be seen what the title implies, in what way *The Compartment* is not synonymous with *The Room*. In a television production of *The Compartment* by the British Broadcasting Corporation on February 20th, 1967, the problem of the title, at least, was solved, as Pinter, who played the part of Stott, changed it simply to *The Basement*. This production showed the obviously visual nature of the script, with dialogue reduced to a minimum and decor becoming instrumental. Furniture and weather have, of course, always been important in Pinter but here the set is almost the major character. The rapid changes in the weather and the furnishings of the flat reflected not merely the passage of time but also the changing emotional relationship of the three characters. The circular nature of the plot is strongly reminiscent of Beckett possibly because of the intended juxtaposition with *Film*, but noticeably the female character played a very passive role contrasting sharply with the emergent female characters Pinter has created in *Tea Party* and *The Homecoming*. And the production could only be achieved by the use of film thus emphasizing the origins of a play not intended for television in the first place. Such film work remains impressive, but it is a distraction from the theater, where Pinter first made a name for himself.[17]

VI *"Tea Party" as a Play*

The short story "Tea Party," first broadcast by the British Broadcasting Corporation and subsequently published in *Playboy* magazine (with the curiously inappropriate epigraph—"in the country of the blind he found himself a king"), was the basis of Pinter's most recent television play of the same name, produced on March 25, 1965. Commissioned by the European Broadcasting Union for "The Largest Theater in the World" and lasting for 75 minutes, *Tea Party* appeared simultaneously in France, Belgium, Luxembourg, Switzerland, Germany, Austria, Spain, Holland, Denmark, Sweden, Norway, and Britain; Italy refused to show it. It took a month to write, and its story was described by Pinter in the *Daily Mirror* (March 26, 1965) as "the story of a businessman's reaction to his new secretary and the effect she has on him. He hires her on the day before his marriage."

This new version of *Tea Party* is about a selfmade businessman, Robert Disson,[18] who, from humble beginnings, has become the head of one of the largest sanitary engineering firms in the country. He hires a new secretary, marries for the second time, and finds that he cannot, literally, believe his own eyes. The original story has been much expanded (the ubiquitous spectacles are not in the visual production); cryptic details in the very short story are filled out in the play; relationships are made more precise; and, in the visual presentation, the division between reality and fantasy is made clearer without destroying the equivocal nature of the experience. More is also made of the social backgrounds of the characters from which the dilemma partly springs.

[138]

VII   Tea Party

The play is Pinter's first full family play. The setting is a spacious office "designed with taste" in Knightsbridge and a spacious house "designed with taste" in St. John's Wood. The season is spring. The action begins with the arrival of Wendy, the new secretary, as she walks down a long, silent, and expensive display of water closets and bidets. For Disson's firm, the making of bidets (and it makes more than anyone else in England) is almost a mission. During the interview, Wendy crosses, uncrosses, and recrosses her legs regularly, and we discover that she left her last job because, understandably, her boss could not stop touching her. Disson, who is mildly affected, hires her and sets her to work on arrangements for his wedding the next day, arrangements that are complicated by a telephone call from his best friend, Disley, a physician, who announces that he has gastric flu and will have to miss the wedding. This raises the problem of best man and the best man's speech, but when Disson discusses this situation with his fiancée, Diana, and her brother, Willy, Willy offers to stand in for Disley. However, as Disson points out, Willy is already giving the bride away and proposing her health at the reception; moreover, Disley's speech was centered on their long friendship. But Diana and Willy agree that neither of these objections matters. At the wedding reception, Willy gives a speech for the bride in which he emphasizes her gracious background and her many talents as the daughter of a politician of apparently some means. He then proposes the health of the groom in a speech that is also about Diana's virtues and graces. Disson's reaction, however, is to offer Willy a job, and the scene fades out on *his* speech, the single phrase that this is the happiest day of his life.

The bedroom scene that follows shows his doubts, however, as he presses Diana to say whether she is happy, a discussion continued the next morning at breakfast before the arrival of the twins (two boys by Disson's previous marriage) in which he presses her to say why she married him and not a Jerry Whatshisname. She says that she did not marry Jerry because he was weak and that she is happy. We then see Disson working happily with his woodwork, constructing a cuckoo clock; but, some time later, again at breakfast, one of the twins calls him "sir," a habit picked up from Uncle Willy that Disson naturally deplores.

Disson shows Willy the office he is to use; it is joined to his own. Both offices are cut off from the rest of the building, and the men's only contact, except for a very rare personal interview, is by intercom. The door between the two offices is, however, kept locked; there is to be no fraternization because, if there is, no work will be done. Yet, when Disson explains his principles, they seem to contradict this physical arrangement. Disson says that he does not like dithering, or selfdoubt, or fuzziness: "Clarity, clear intention, precise execution." Living for him is a matter of active and willing participation (by intercom presumably?): "Nothing is more sterile or lamentable than the man content to live within himself." He insists that it is essential to cultivate the ability to operate lucidly on problems and therefore be in a position to solve them; it is, he says, Willy's job to understand him, and his to understand Willy. All this conversation is ironic in view of the situation as revealed so far, not to mention how the rest of the play reveals it. When Willy asks for Diana as his secretary, Disson rather curiously agrees.

A short scene between the twins and Diana suggests that adjustments have been made and are working well. But beneath their politeness, the twins seem remote beings. In the next scene, we begin to explore Disson's relationship with his secretary—the first signs of an intimate relationship. It is no accident that after this first contact, when, as Wendy says, she will have no difficulty in meeting his requirements, Disson sees double while playing ping-pong with Willy. But Disley can find nothing wrong with his eyes; indeed, Disson, by describing the office minutely, shows that his eyesight is excellent. However, he still cannot tie his tie accurately. When Willy and Diana praise Wendy for being the perfect secretary, he cannot control his irritation—an irritation accompanied by a natural mistrust of his wife as a secretary, since he suspects that she is exposed, even with her brother, to the same treatment as Wendy. In a woodwork scene with the boys (who would prefer to study the Middle Ages—one of the many puns in the play), Disson is so uncertain that he nearly cuts one of the boy's fingers off.

By this time eyeweakness, as well as the need for Wendy's chiffon scarf tied round his face to protect his eyes, is established as the context in which Disson at the office can explore her body. But, when Willy borrows her, and Disson, on his knees trying to peer through the keyhole of the door, is caught by his wife, who is supposed to have gone home, there is a moment, the only one, of actual physical anger. Disson excuses his behavior by pretending to have been looking for his pencil, but assuming the innocence of Willy, Wendy, and Diana, his behavior must look highly embarrassing and suspicious. He, of course, suspects that Willy is taking liberties not merely with his wife but also with his secretary. An elaborate football game between Disson and Wendy played with a table lighter contrasts sharply with a subdued bedroom scene between Disson and his wife. Preparations are made to celebrate their first anniversary with a tea party at the office, but a total blackout in the next scene, shared by the viewers, is seen by Wendy as an excuse for Disson to play games and to be naughty again.

Disley very rightly hints that he needs help; however, it is not his eyes that are at fault. In a scene with Diana and Willy in which Disson discusses his background and theirs, something of the cause emerges tantalizingly. Disson remembers his old life: "I used to down eleven or nine pints a night! Eleven or nine pints! Every night of the stinking week! Me and the boys! The boys! And me! I'd break any man's hand for . . . for playing me false. That was before I became a skilled craftsman." This picture contrasts sharply with the life at Sunderley for Diana and Willy, with its lake, long windows, drawing room, music, swans, and owls. When Disson has to ask once more why Diana married him, she replies: "I found you admirable in your clarity of mind, your surety of purpose, your will, the strength your achievements had given you." Jerry, we remember, was rejected because he was weak. Disson's behavior alarms Willy, but Disson brushes this alarm aside and promptly makes him a partner. In the next scene, the two partners go to a business luncheon, and the two secretaries meet and go away together, presumably to discuss why men will touch them. At the second game of ping-pong, Disson has a total blackout.

Disson's parents arrive for the anniversary. They are ordinary people, and Pinter exactly captures in his dialogue the latent embarrassments that arise out of the two aspects of Disson—his plebian past and his present affluence. Perhaps their arrival

makes Disson even more uncertain, for, in the next scene he rejects Wendy's chiffon and insists that Disley come and tie a
bandage round his eyes. From this point, the play shifts into
rapid shots as the guests arrive for the tea party—Mr. and Mrs.
Disley, Disson's parents, the twins, Diana, Willy, and Wendy.
Obviously, a television production depends largely on visual appeal, and this one is remarkable for its combination of acting
and camera work. A brief piece of dialogue, in itself almost
meaningless, is constantly illuminated by the sort of shot that
would require a chapter in a novel.

The critics treated the play respectfully. Mary Crozier, in *The
Guardian* (March 26, 1965) thought it "a very good play, indeed, written with extraordinary definition and clarity, and yet
with all those strange undertones of the sinister and the absurd
of which he is a master." Eric Shorter, in *The Daily Telegraph*
(March 26, 1965) found Pinter at the top of his teasing form
with plenty of effects and implications, while Maurice Wiggin,
in *The Sunday Times* (March 28, 1965) did not understand the
play but liked it as a piece of powerful, brilliant writing from
which meaning would later emerge. On the other hand, Maurice
Richardson, in *The Observer* (March 28, 1965) found it devil-
ish clever but "a simple rather shallow piece, with a story a fly
could follow" and noted the ample use of fetish and symbol
while rejecting a Swiss television critic's view of it as a national
allegory (he apparently saw it as representing English business
men). The weekly press critics naturally had longer to compose
notices. Patrick Anderson, in *The Spectator* (April 2, 1965) saw
the appropriateness of Disson's purging society of its waste products and his inability to purge the subconscious, but he also
found the play altogether too much of a case history—"more
menace than life," a view partially supported by John Holstrom,
in *The New Statesman* (April 2, 1965), who thought the central
character unconvincingly presented as a man of achievement.
Holstrom—believing that Pinter is still the *miglior fabbro* of contemporary dramatists and that he has raised television drama in
plays like *The Collection* and *The Lover* to a remarkable pitch
of concentration while remaining graceful, ironic, and entertaining—was a little disappointed; to him, the play was "intriguing,
funny in parts, sexy in parts, never entirely satisfactory." He
thought the play rambled.

However much time a critic had to prepare his review, no one was perhaps as precise and detailed as the anonymous critic of *The Times* (March 26, 1965). He pointed out that we once more had a Pinter play about a sanctuary—the vast modern office building barricaded by wealth and power but resting on plumbing—and a hero still beset by some obscure dread. The long deserted corridors, the locked offices, and the former self of Disson exact revenge for his success. He marries a politician's daughter, engages her brother in his business, but is attacked by doubts and blindness. He finally collapses at the office tea party and retreats into a catatonic trance, the most complete sanctuary. This critic noted the use of fetishes—leather, high heels—and saw the play as a game of mutual provocation between Disson and his secretary: they defy the icily dehumanized setting.

A critic's work is more difficult in regard to a television play than when dealing with a film; *Tea Party* was shown once only, a film can be seen several times. Certain ideas emerge from seeing the play, however. After Disley has warned the guests that Disson's eyes are strained but that they must not embarrass him by speaking of it, the play was divided, visually, into two kinds of shots: Disson's point of view (what he thinks is happening) and shots that include Disson (and are presumably what is happening). Disson's point of view was soundless action, reflecting the tensions that have been built up in the play, but the other shots show the normal, if strained, atmosphere of a tea party. When Disson "sees" Willy pile cushions on Wendy's desk and help both Wendy and Diana onto them and then "sees" Willy begin to caress them, he collapses and hears nothing—not even Diana's closing words: ". . . It's your wife." The play ends on a close-up of Disson's open eyes.

This ending, as the critic in *The Listener* (April 15, 1965) pointed out, is the crisis of the play and could have been the beginning of another. But it is unlikely that a dramatist would try to send the audience out at such a moment from the theater. This comment notes the difference between television and the theater, and it would not be likely to lead to any conclusion. But, if we read this final collapse as a kind of death totally unexpected by the innocent bystanders, then it forms a conventional sort of ending, admittedly one lacking the restoration of order, but also one avoiding the customary distribution of prizes or moral statement (and this latter the play ought to have done if there is to be one).

We can offer certain explanations of the play. Disson marries above himself to stabilize his place in upper-class society. But his real character guiltily shows itself with Wendy—his behavior, as he himself says, is something that only takes place in paperback books, not in life. Class warfare, success, relationships that collapse, all center on a hero who tries to conceal them in more trivial failures—an inability to play ping-pong or do woodwork. But eventually his suspicions, jealousy, and the recognition or fear of inadequacy reduce him to the condition forced on Edward in *A Slight Ache*. Although the reasons are different, it is noticeable that Edward, too, married the squire's daughter in order to rise in the world. But in *Tea Party*, the relationships are, for the first time, explored in a family—a family of several generations, which looks forward to *The Homecoming*. The group of characters remains, however, small. As with all his television plays from *A Night Out* onward, sex is firmly in the Pinter world, and crucially so. Disson becomes suspicious of every relationship: with his best friend (in the story nothing so precise as gastric flu accounts for that friend's inability to attend the wedding, nor is it specified that best man and physician are the same); with his wife, whom he cannot believe really wants to marry him—he even suspects her of being too closely related to her brother (the remark about playing brother and sister at Sunderley is both ambiguous and sinister); with his twin sons, who, always polite, seem to menace and mock him more and more as the play proceeds; and with Wendy, with whom his game is played in the dark and whom he suspects of being unfaithful to him with Willy. Even Diana and Wendy are suspected of a perverted relationship in one scene.

In this world of the successful, the well-bred, and the self-made, sickness and isolation remain the problem. Curiously, the more family there is, and the more success there is, the more isolated and suspicious Disson seems to be. The play covers a longer period of time than is usual—one year—with no precise indications of how rapidly the breakdown takes place. This development should have been more clearly indicated, since a short play presents a long, slow process perhaps too rapidly for an audience's credulity. The blindness itself—a blank screen flecked with grey-white patches—captures the feelings of Disson very well, just as close-ups suggest isolation by cutting everything else out and underline tensions and insecurity. The symbolic objects —water closets, bidets, ping-pong ball, and mirrors—are aligned with shots of a fetishistic nature (leather, black chiffon, high heels) and incorporated in scenes like the football game with the table lighter (which at one point lay at Wendy's feet like an apple!) or a game of chess in order to give the play a brilliant but evasive patina, suggesting that we cannot be entirely sure that the whole thing is not completely the delusion of Disson's guilty, secret, true self.

CHAPTER 6

The Homecoming

THE NIGHT AFTER the British Broadcasting Corporation production of *Tea Party*, the Royal Shakespeare Company presented, in Cardiff, Pinter's most recent stage play, *The Homecoming*. After a short provincial tour, the play entered the repertoire at the Aldwych in June, 1965. Directed by Peter Hall, the cast included Vivien Merchant playing the part of Ruth.

I *Substance*

The Homecoming is a summer play that belies its weather; its action would seem more suitable to the winter of *The Room* and of *The Caretaker*. Set in an old Victorian house in north London, the play can be seen as a series of bouts in a battle that is mainly verbal but which occasionally becomes physical violence. Each member of the family looks to his own advantage, using what weapons—cunning, virility, intelligence, even authority (as the father does, for example)—he or she possesses. Perception of the structure of the play as a series of fights to discover who can most successfully dominate whom will not, however, explain the play. There are the characters of Sam and Teddy who have questionable kinds of virtues, to be fitted in. And "virtue" is a word to be used most circumspectly at this point, or any other, in relation to the play.

The opening scene is between a taciturn Lenny (he is trying to read a newspaper) and his aggressively talkative father, Max. Their relationship is suggested in the following exchange:

LENNY: Plug it, will you, you stupid sod, I'm trying to read the paper.
MAX: Listen! I'll chop your spine off, you talk to me like that! You understand? Talking to your lousy filthy father like that!
LENNY: You know what, you're getting demented.

Max, stimulated by a query about horse-racing advanced by Lenny only to annoy him, romances, or tells the truth, about the time when he was young and a rebel with his friend Macgregor and about his gift with horses, denied fulfillment because of family obligations. When Lenny taunts him, Max raises his stick, but Lenny only mocks the gesture with a little boy's voice. Max's violence is ineffectual and curtailed even before Uncle Sam arrives. Sam is quietly "sent up" by his nephew Lenny, who both taunts Sam on his qualities of politeness, courtesy, and efficiency as a driver and excludes Max from the conversation— thus achieving the maximum amount of irritation at the expense of both his father and his uncle. When Lenny tires of the game, he leaves, and Max immediately starts to sneer at Sam's gifts, which have not included women and virility but which do include niceness and a conventional attitude toward women, marriage, and life in general. This episode is itself curtailed by the arrival of another son, Joey, whose innocent remark that he is hungry goads Max into a bitter diatribe about the mess he finds himself in. When Joey tactfully goes upstairs to be out of the way, Max returns to the attack on Sam. Sam insists on speaking well of Max's late wife, Jessie, whom he characterizes as a perfect lady, but he damns Max's friend Macgregor in a brutal, brisk way. Max, who turns savagely on him, threatens to throw him out when he ceases to be economically useful. Sam reminds him that it is their mother's house, their father's house, and the scene ends with Max's bitter reminiscences of his father provoked by this reminder.

Scene Two introduces the eldest son, Teddy, who, with his wife Ruth, is returning from abroad very early in the morning. From the beginning, these two seem to be at odds with each other, although less definably and more importantly, than the Sandses in *The Room*. They disagree on such simple matters as staying with the family or not and staying up or going to bed; they change attitudes without knowing why; and Teddy seems unduly insistent that Ruth should not be afraid of his family, who are nice warm people. Ruth finally goes out for a walk, and Lenny enters. However, after six years' separation, the two brothers have nothing more important to talk about than Lenny's insomnia and the tick of his clock; and, as Teddy goes to bed, he declines a glass of water offered by his hospitable brother. Ruth returns, and she also discusses Lenny's tick, Venice, the difference in things between day and night—all in an interested if irrelevant manner—until Lenny gives her a glass of water and asks if he can touch her. When Ruth asks why (thus echoing Wendy and Diana in *Tea Party*), she is told a long story about a society lady who took liberties with Lenny down by the docks and got kicked because he had decided she was diseased. Lenny's sensitivity, which apparently is the point of this story, is explained by a further anecdote concerning an old lady and her mangle. She too was violently beaten up by Lenny.

Lenny then challenges Ruth by moving the ash tray, which she is not using, and then by trying to take away her glass, but she counterattacks, making suggestions to him which so alarm him that she finishes her drink and goes to bed while he is still trying to figure out what sort of proposal has been made to him. He does this so noisily that he awakens Max, who comes down and naturally wants to know whom he is hiding. This demand for an explanation is countered by Lenny's asking for information about whether or not he was intended on the night of his conception. Since Max is silent, Lenny muses on why he did not ask his dear mother. At the mention of Jessie, Max spits at him, and the scene ends with a joke about having to vacuum the carpet.

The third scene is after breakfast early in the morning. Joey is doing push-ups in front of the mirror. Max, curiously resentful of Sam, who is washing up in the kitchen, finally calls him in and attacks him—for harboring resentment against Max! The familiar complaints against Sam are listed—his lack of violence and greed —and only the arrival of Teddy and Ruth in dressing gowns curtails this episode. Max feels like a fool, because his son has so casually returned without his knowing it; he attacks Ruth, calling her a dirty tart and a filthy scrubber; and he finally tells Joey to throw her out. Joey, however, merely tells his father that he is an old man and is promptly punched in the belly for saying so. The effort overwhelms Max; he begins to collapse, and Sam hurries forward to help him. Max hits Sam over the head with his stick and sinks breathless onto the couch. Suddenly Max speaks quite normally to Ruth to ask her if she has any children, and he greets Teddy with great affection, inviting him to kiss and cuddle his father. Teddy accepts, and the act ends with Max's declaration that Teddy still loves his father. The sentimental, strained emotionalism of this scene could perhaps be explained, as could the atmosphere, say, in Peter Shaffer's *Five Finger Exercise*, if the family were Jewish; but it is nowhere suggested that they are. It should also be noted that this emotionalism is as ironic and savage as anything else in the play. Teddy is, in fact, offering to punch his father if he does come for that kiss and cuddle!

Act Two opens with a long tableau of the family assembled for coffee after lunch. Max leers charmingly at Ruth, who compliments him on the lunch. He compliments her on the coffee and, in this saccharine atmosphere of *bonhomie*, becomes nostalgic as he regrets that Jessie, his dead wife, and the grandchildren (Teddy's sons in America) are not there so that she could make a fuss over them. He talks nostalgically of an episode in his own life with Jessie and their sons, but the charming family scene is rapidly replaced by the more brutal and succinct one of a crippled family, three bastard sons, and a bitch of a wife. In this more customary vein, Max returns to insulting Sam on the usual grounds of his weakness, courtesy, lack of virility (i.e., violence), and idleness. Sam, insulted, leaves for work, after first shaking hands with Ruth courteously. Max then initiates a discussion about Ruth as a good cook and a good wife, and he gives Ruth and Teddy, rather belatedly, his blessing. Teddy supports this gracious picture of Ruth by describing their happy life in America in a flourishing university in a successful department —a picture Ruth immediately qualifies with the hesitant suggestion that she was different before she met Teddy. Teddy's too hasty rejection of this qualification produces a situation that is apparently avoided by Lenny's discussion of philosophy. This philosophical inquiry—into the nature of a table (in order to bait Teddy, whose Ph.D. is, surprisingly, in philosophy) and what to do with it when one has taken it—is dissolving into laughter because of the suggestions of Max (sell it) and Joey (chop it up for firewood) when Ruth completely alters the tone by substituting her leg and underwear for the table as the object of consideration. This reminder of her physical presence, coupled with *her* view of America as all rocks and insects, produces another embarrassed silence. And the family leaves in a quiet, brisk, but orderly manner.

It is now Teddy, and not Ruth, who wishes to go straight back to America, pushing the claims of his own family, recognizing that there are two families—his family here (father, uncle, brothers) and his other family (three children in America). He contrasts the cleanness of America with the dirt of north London.

When he leaves to pack, Lenny enters, discussing the change in the weather and the need for new winter clothes. Ruth once more focuses attention on her body by asking him to admire her shoes (and, incidentally, her legs). She tells him of her life as a photographer's model before she married Teddy and how she used to go to the country to a large house with a lake. She describes how she went there before she left for America with Teddy, saw the house brilliant with light, but was shut out. Teddy returns with her coat and the suitcases, but she accepts Lenny's offer to dance, and she is kissing him when Joey and Max return. As Joey says, Teddy really has married a tart, and to prove it, he takes over from Lenny, lying on top of her on the couch while Lenny strokes her hair. Max unconcernedly discusses Teddy's departure and Ruth as a woman of feeling. Teddy says and does nothing.

Abruptly, the mood changes. Ruth, by now on the floor with Joey, pushes him aside and asks for food and a drink. She insists on having her whisky in a tumbler and, suddenly, attacks Teddy on the subject of his critical works. These the family have never seen and, according to Teddy, would not understand: "You're just objects. You just . . . move about. I can observe it. I can see what you do. It's the same as I do. But you're lost in it. You won't get me being . . . I won't be lost in it."[1] It is difficult to see whether we are supposed to sympathize with Teddy's point of view or not. An attack by the family on Teddy's selfishness and lack of family-feeling moves easily into an attack on the American way of life by Lenny, who appeals for grace, generosity of mind, and liberality of spirit.

At this point, Joey, who has been upstairs with Ruth during Lenny's attack on Teddy, comes down, and the men discuss whether or not Ruth is a tease. Anecdotes are told to support the view that Joey is excessively attractive to girls, but Teddy seems unmoved. Even when the family decides it would like to keep Ruth by setting her up as a prostitute, Teddy remains unconcerned. He is moved to neither anger nor action by Lenny's suggestion that he should pimp for them in America, although he does decline to support Ruth if she stays. Sam's reminder that Teddy and Ruth are married is ignored.

When Ruth comes down, Teddy explains the plan to her. She considers it and then accepts it on her own terms, which show that she is as shrewd on the economic angle as Lenny. Sam's doubtful intervention, revealing that Jessie had been unfaithful with Macgregor, is brushed aside as the product of a diseased imagination and his collapse is ignored. Teddy is moved only to regret that Sam cannot now drive him to the airport, which shows him as one of the family, after all; and after discussing trains and taxis with his father, he leaves with Ruth's curious injunction not to become a stranger as their only farewell.

The play ends as Joey lies with his head on Ruth's lap. Max, after hinting that she will use them, drops his stick and crawls to her, protesting that he is not old and asking for a kiss. Lenny looks on, enigmatically aloof. This final tableau is one of a mother with her children. Ruth has, in fact, come home—or found it amidst the alien corn. The lack of sympathy for conventional goodness and morality is simply a suggestion that they are not at home here. Respectable life in this dark world is the ultimate illusion. Inside the room, even dreams are savage, violent, sexual, and powerful. Ruth has come home to the family she merits and which deserves her; or, put without moral overtones, she is where she belongs.

II   *Criticism of* The Homecoming

There were very few reviews of the play while it was still on its provincial run. Benedict Nightingale, in *The Guardian* (March 27, 1965), found that Pinter's message of greed and violence in everyday places had never seemed more uncompromisingly nasty, but, surprisingly, the play was funny. The critic of *The Daily Express* (April 3, 1965) defined Pinter's technique as expressing an appalling situation with "innocent understatement," while the critic of *The Manchester Evening News* (April 3, 1965) found some of it vaguely distasteful.

When the play opened in London, the reviewers were respectful but not entirely enthusiastic. *The Guardian* (June 5, 1965) said that the play was perfectly turned, but to what end?—a view shared by many other critics. Most interesting, perhaps, was the allegorical interpretation by David Benedictus in *The Spectator* (June 11, 1965), who read the play as biography: Teddy (= Pinter away from the stage for six years) with his wife (= work) returns to his family (= his public)—and, he concluded, Pinter has not come home. Probably the most satisfactory critique appeared in *Encore* (July-August, 1965) and was written by Stuart Hall. He pointed out the necessity for a large, bare set (in a more cluttered environment, these characters would have eaten one another long ago) and that language is still a form of noncommunication. What keeps the family going is a constant sense of threat, sustained by verbal assaults. The twist to the play is not Teddy's defeat, but Ruth's betrayal, and Hall feels that the long speech by Teddy is very important. What Teddy proposes may be virtues, but only in another setting. Teddy goes in for linguistic indulgence—and while he is modifying his verbs, Joey and Lenny are operating on and with Ruth. The family needs a woman and gets one. Hall sees the whole play, therefore, as exposing the machinery of fantasy. Teddy loses because his fantasies are remote.

Most critics were respectful, possibly because they had learned their lesson in criticizing *The Birthday Party*. On one point concerning *The Homecoming* they were all rightly troubled —the lack of moral content. Where does Pinter go from this black fable? Consideration of *The Homecoming* can be divided under three general headings: the family, morality, and philosophy. Each of these is a key to the play.

III *The Family*

The setting of the play is a room in a large house. Everybody has his own room in it, but the family meets in the living room, the back wall of which has been knocked down to make a larger area. In fact, the living room has become a hall. This architectural alteration took place when the mother died, and the reference in the play would seem to suggest that the new room and the death of the mother, Jessie, have something more than a joke in common. The mother-father relationship is repeated twice in the play because *The Homecoming* is about generations. In spite of family ties, relationships are strained or nonexistent throughout the play. The family, in fact, is a group of individuals who emerge at certain times from their own rooms.

Obviously, familiar Pinter devices spring to mind with this play: the possession of a room, failure to communicate, subterranean violence, intruding forces, and women who are at the

same time mother, wife, and whore. This is the first family
Pinter has put on the stage, although he anticipates a large
family in *Tea Party*, and the action takes in four generations, if
we include the grandparents and grandchildren with whom the
characters are concerned. But the play is not precisely about the
difference between generations; it concerns the bonds that
separate and unite what is conventionally a single unit. The alien
force that intrudes is at home: Teddy, who has gotten out of the
room at last, cannot resist coming back; and Ruth already belongs to the district and class. Their alien quality is stressed by
America and Teddy's Ph.D.

Sam and Max, as brothers, seem curiously unalike; and the
relationship between two dissimilar brothers does not exist between them as it does in *The Caretaker*. Yet, in a sense, they are
both facets of the same character. Max is domineering, lecherous,
aggressive, and contemptuous of his brother Sam. Sam seems
ineffectual yet virtuous. Only as the play proceeds does Sam begin to emerge as a doubtful character. His attitude toward women, and particularly toward Jessie, whom he may have admired
so much as to remain single, is sharply contradicted by the facts
as he knows them—and, from the audience's point of view, by the
women of the play. Jessie was, apparently, unfaithful; and Ruth
is a tease, a nymphomaniac, or both. The women in the anecdotes intensify the shadowy lady in Aston's story in *The Caretaker*—diseased, domineering, or simple vehicles for lust (the
society woman, the old lady with her mangle and the "birds" at
the Scrubs).

Sam's conventional reminder, when Max threatens to throw
him out as soon as he ceases to be economically useful, that they
are brothers in their father's house only produces an equivocal
remembrance of that father from Max: "Our father? I remember
him. Don't worry. You kid yourself. He used to come over to me
and look down at me. My old man did. He'd bend right over me,
then he'd pick me up. I was only that big. Then he'd dandle me.
Give me the bottle, wipe me clean. Give me a smile. Pat me on
the bum. Catch me coming down. I remember my father."[2]

Yet when it suits Max, when he is attacking Sam, he can evoke
the sacred memory of that father: "I respected my father not
only as a man but as a number one butcher! And to prove it I
followed him into the shop, I learned to carve a carcass at his

knee, I commemorated his name in blood, I gave birth to three grown men! All on my own bat. What have you done?"[3] In Act Two, Max remembers the family after his father's death, when, as he says, he had to look after his bedridden mother and his invalid brothers who needed psychiatrists; here there is a conflict between his *family* and *his* family.

His family is Jessie and three sons, and they, too, emerge equivocally: Jessie is both a sacred memory and a whore. Max's first reference to her, when he is talking to Lenny, is: "Mind you, she wasn't such a bad woman. Even though it made me sick just to look at her rotten stinking face she wasn't such a bad bitch. I gave her the best bleeding years of my life, anyway."[4] Since he refers to himself in the next breath as "your lousy filthy father," it is difficult to see how endearing or not such speeches can be. Max maintains during his long monologue on horses that his family obligations prevented him from becoming a trainer for one of the dukes, but it may well be that his only association with horses (in the light of that group of butchers with Continental associations) was for their meat. He apparently suspects Macgregor and Jessie, but when Sam confirms the suspicions at the end of the play, Max brushes him aside, dismissing the idea as the product of Sam's diseased imagination. When Sam eulogizes Jessie's qualities as a lady and companion, Max's only response is a quiet but exasperated "Christ!". When Joey asks for food and Max sarcastically asks if he is their mother, he is being sarcastic at Joey's expense, as usual, but the remark may also reflect his natural frustration at being reduced to the role of housekeeper for his sons.

His relationship with these sons is as full of tensions and ambivalences as his memories of his parents, his wife, and his relationship with his brother. We are told in a savage passage that Max loved to tuck the boys in bed and, later, what fun it was to give them baths. The first act ends with the embarrassing invitation to Teddy to have a kiss and a cuddle, which clearly reflects a childhood habit; but his attack on Joey as a useless boxer, and his anger when Lenny mockingly calls him "Dad" several times, produce a contradiction in the play. The first typical exchange between Lenny and Max, already cited, bears repeating to remind us of how matters seem to stand:

LENNY: Plug it, will you, you stupid sod, I'm trying to read the paper.

MAX: Listen! I'll chop your spine off, you talk to me like that! You understand? Talking to your lousy filthy father like that!

LENNY: You know what, you're getting demented.[5]

We cannot write off this dialogue or that of the whole play simply as affectionate abuse.

When Teddy arrives, he is obviously uneasy about introducing his wife to the family, which is, apparently, after six years, still unaware that he is married and has three children. He wants to slip into his old room and postpone the meeting until the next day. Why he is afraid of this introduction is not clear, although having seen the family, it is understandable and, in the light of Ruth's behavior, justifiable, but it becomes clear that the real root of the problem is the relationship between Teddy and Ruth. His description of the room and the structural alterations following his mother's death seem to suggest something. And we can reasonably ask why Ruth and Teddy spent a week in Venice before coming to visit the family. When Teddy and Lenny meet, they have nothing to discuss except the tick of Lenny's clock. And why is Lenny so upset when Ruth, countering his proposals, calls him "Leonard," the name his mother gave him? Either he loves it (her) or hates it (her)? At any rate, Lenny does not tell his father that the prodigal has returned with a wife. Instead, he attacks his father on the subject of his conception; he wants to know if he was intended to be conceived:

I'm only asking this in a spirit of inquiry, you understand that, don't you? I'm curious. And there's lots of people of my age share that curiosity, you know that, Dad? They often ruminate, sometimes single, sometimes in groups, about the true facts of that particular night—the night they were made in the image of those two people *at it*. It's a question long overdue, from my point of view, but as we happen to be passing the time of day here tonight I thought I'd pop it to you.[6]

The mention of the dead mother only makes Max spit at Lenny. Max's anger at not knowing about Teddy's return is more understandable if we realize that he knows or suspects that Lenny has concealed it from him. But it does not entirely explain the manner of the attack, his accusing Ruth of being a dirty tart, or the ironies of his confused syntax: "I've never had a whore under this roof before. Ever since your mother died. My word of honour. (*To* JOEY.) Have you ever had a whore here? Has Lenny ever had a whore here? They come back from America, they bring the slopbucket with them. They bring the bedpan with them. (*To* TEDDY.) Take that disease away from me. Get her away from me."[7]

The second act shows the family gathered after lunch. The members arrange themselves like a Victorian photograph and exhibit the family pieties such a photograph was intended to convey. This cozy assembly leads to nostalgic reminiscing on Max's part; he wishes he could have both Jessie and the grandchildren there so that she could fuss over them. It was Jessie, Max asserts, who was the backbone of the family and who taught the boys all the morality they know—an ambiguous compliment under the circumstances. He pursues the idyllic picture to remember the night he was entering a business association with a group of butchers and pampered Jessie and the boys: "I remember the boys came down, in their pyjamas, all their hair shining, their faces pink, it was before they started shaving, and they knelt down at our feet, Jessie's and mine. I tell you it was like Christmas."[8] But Ruth probes the idyl with an economic question about the butchers, who, like everyone else, turned out to be a bunch of criminals. The picture alters rapidly with Max's terse summary of his situation—a bedridden mother, invalid brothers, "three bastard sons, a slutbitch of a wife," and a "lazy idle bugger" of a brother.

Teddy appears to have the same problem of definition. His picture of life in America with his marvelous wife, three sons, and a successful department is immediately challenged by Ruth. When the family leaves husband and wife together, Teddy's attempts to get Ruth to leave seem curiously halfhearted. Even Venice, to which he took her, has become for her an echo of Lenny's previous speech. The discussion with Lenny about right shoes (right for *what?*)—so reminiscent of Davies in *The Caretaker*—leads her to reveal what she says her former life was, to describe the attractions of modeling in country houses with bright lights. These bright lights, necessary for photography, also symbolize the glamor of that life as opposed to her life now as housewife and a mother who helps her husband to write his lectures.

Occasionally, Teddy does behave like a member of the family; he eats Lenny's cheese roll, for example, which leads Lenny into a discussion of Teddy as a member of the family. In America, Lenny suggests, Teddy has grown less outgoing and more sulky, almost into an individual who contrasts to the unity of family:

> But nevertheless we do make up a unit, Teddy, and you're an integral part of it. When we all sit round the back yard having a quiet gander at the night sky, there's always an empty chair standing in the circle which is in fact yours. And so when you at length return to us, we do expect a bit of grace, a bit of je ne sais quoi, a bit of generosity of mind, a bit of liberality of spirit, to reassure us. We do expect that. But do we get it? Have we got it? Is that what you've given us?[9]

Teddy's short answer—"yes"—is probably truthful. He has, however, refused to accept the family even when it takes his wife and accepts her as mother, wife, and whore. Sam's revelation about Jessie can be ignored, but Ruth can warn Teddy not to become a stranger.

IV The Morality

This invitation to Teddy not to be a stranger to his family is, perhaps, the moral crux of the play, although clearly the whole matter of the play is not merely shocking, but seriously disturbing. From the average point of view, we are confronted with material and a plot out of Zola or Dreiser which are treated like a comedy of manners. In fact, *The Homecoming* is a kind of contemporary Restoration comedy where the vernacular wit should compel us into some sort of point of view from which a moral judgment is inappropriate. Becoming a stranger from one's family (treated with such sympathy in *Tea Party*) almost becomes in *The Homecoming* a necessary and heroic deed when the family has so little to redeem itself.

The characters represent the violent, bloody aspects of life: Max is a butcher; Joey, a demolition man and spare-time boxer; and Lenny, a pimp. Jessie, the mother, was, apparently, grossly unfaithful. The third son, a Ph.D., returns from America with a wife whom he had married hurriedly and secretly six years before and who has borne him three sons. He brings her back to his family, makes no protest when she is insulted, and watches unconcernedly while she barters her body as if it were a desirable corner site. Max's greeting in Act Two—"Where's the whore? Still in bed? She'll make us all animals"—evokes no response from anyone, including her husband. In short, no one shows any concern. There is a great deal of talk about family affection, but every memory of childhood evoked is immediately contradicted, and all the characters show themselves to be self-seeking, violent, and selfish.

The play entertains, although it is noticeable that what produces laughter differs from person to person even more decidedly than with the average comedy. At times, it is difficult to decide how far the laughter is caused by sheer disbelief or by hysteria. But if we compare a recent "black" comedy, Joe Orton's *Loot* (which was dropped after a provincial tour and only opened a year or so later in London) with Pinter's *The Homecoming*, the latter seems to involve deeper if undefined issues; or, put another way, it gives an impression that there are such issues involved. Both plays deal with greed and violence, and neither play is at all interested in social reform or in the correction of social abuses by laughter. Because *The Homecoming* did create the impression of saying something and because it does involve the audience in a rich, violent, and horrid situation, the need for a point of reference becomes more pressing. Orton's *Loot* is a tale of intrigue and counterintrigue by totally amoral, greedy people, but Pinter's *The Homecoming* from its very title implies a situation in which certain prejudices will be tested.

The most serious of these is the concept of the family itself. Teddy's refusal to be "lost" in the family issue is a good one, but it is qualified by his willingness to lose his wife in it, and his brutal indifference to Sam's collapse shows how truly he is a member of his family. If he has chosen *his* family (his sons) and if the choice is a right one, he ought to be more strongly concerned with keeping his lawful wife as well. Instead, he seems to lose himself in philosophical speculation, which, indeed, makes him a stranger to this particular family.

V *The Philosophical Center*

Stuart Hall, in his review of the play (*Encore*, July-August, 1965) suggested the importance of Teddy's long speech as the philosophical center of the play. But Lenny, too, has long speeches that are not simply anecdotes. The philosophical threads are strongly reminiscent of the arguments in *The Dwarfs*. The first obvious absurdity is that Teddy has a Ph.D. in philosophy. The family constantly harps on its pleasure at having a doctor in the house, but, in the action of the play, it is Lenny who speculates. Teddy seems to be philosophical only in the contemptible sense of the word. Lenny, rather than his father, seems to be obsessed with order and clarity. He, unlike the rest of the family, has his study downstairs; he is sensitive to atmosphere, and only becomes desensitized when *unreasonable* demands are made on him; and he says he wants the *true facts* about his conception. All these are in context, of course, which may qualify the reasons behind them. But it is Lenny who, on his first meeting with Teddy, and later with Ruth, speculates on the sameness and difference of things, and in the following passage Lenny is surely arguing like a philosopher:

I mean there are lots of things which tick in the night, don't you find that? All sorts of objects, which, in the day, you wouldn't call anything else but commonplace. They give you no trouble, but in the night any given one of a number of them is liable to start letting out a bit of a tick. Whereas you look at these objects in the day and they're just commonplace. They're quiet as mice during the daytime. So . . . all things being equal . . . this question of me saying it was the clock that woke me up, well, that could very easily prove something of a false hypothesis.[10]

And it is Lenny, in Act Two, who mockingly probes Teddy's philosophy. Teddy's philosophy seems to be incredibly academic and narrow; his rejection of "logical incoherence in the central affirmations of Christian theism" as outside his province is reasonable, as is perhaps Lenny's discussion of what merits reverence: "Well, look at it this way. How can the unknown merit reverence? In other words, how can you revere that of which you are ignorant? At the same time, it would be ridiculous to propose that what we *know* merits reverence. What we know merits any one of a number of things, but it stands to reason reverence isn't one of them. In other words, apart from the known and the unknown what else is there?"[11] Teddy declines to answer, but surely the business of being and not being ought to fall within a philosopher's province? When he philosophically pronounces a table is a table, Lenny ironically appeals to Joey in admiration of this certainty! Even Ruth's excursion into philosophy is more creative. Mention of Teddy's "critical works" would perhaps indicate that he practices noncreative contemporary philosophy, which is analytical and narrow and completely opposed to the wider-ranging questions and ideas of the more Existentialist Lenny. Teddy has never sent his critical works to the family:

You wouldn't understand my works. You wouldn't have the faintest idea of what they were about. You wouldn't appreciate the points of reference. You're way behind. All of you. There's no point in my sending you my works. (*Breathless.*) You'd be lost. It's nothing to do with the question of intelligence. It's a way of being able to look at the world. It's a question of how far you can operate on things (*Hoarse.*) and not in things. I mean it's a question of your capacity to ally the two, to relate the two, to balance the two. To see, to be able to see! I'm the one who can see. That's why I can write my critical works. Might do you good . . . have a look at them . . . see how certain people can view (*Feverish.*) . . . things . . . how certain people can maintain . . . intellectual equilibrium. Intellectual equilibrium. You're just objects. You just . . . move about. I can observe it. I can see what you do. It's the same as I do. But you're lost in it. You won't get me being . . . I won't be lost in it.[12]

Although this speech is remarkably moving, its effect is momentary, unlike Aston's long speech in *The Caretaker.* It tells us very little about Teddy except that he is as cold and as ruthless as the rest of his family.

VI *Some Conclusions About* The Homecoming

Terms like "comedy" and "tragedy" are, of course, not very applicable to such a play as *The Homecoming*; however, if the play is to have a label, tragedy seems nearer the truth. But then the question remains: whose tragedy? If all life is a battle (for possession of *what* is not made clear), the crucial relationship, drawn from *The Collection* and *The Lover*, is between the "sensitive" Teddy (who is inhumanly insensitive) and his wife Ruth after six years of marriage. As in *Tea Party*, sex is central, and violence has returned to the stage, re-established physically as well as verbally, but more subtly than in *The Room* and more horribly than in Mick's practical jokes in *The Caretaker*.

The characters, as usual, tell us very little whether they are extremely silent (Sam, Joey, Teddy, and Ruth) or loquacious (Max and Lenny), and long monologues are mainly avoided. Characters reminisce or relate anecdotes briskly, with near-irrelevance at times, truthfully or not; and the truth is less important than their contribution to the total atmosphere of the play—disease, blood, violence, sex, and power. If the exposition is more subtle and economical than in, say, Aston's long monologue in *The Caretaker*, the nastiness of the experience related is nowhere compensated for by our being sympathetically affected. Society is nowhere indicted: "innocent understatement" nicely describes the distance from the situation at which the play puts us. But, if the action has become simple violence or elaborate and cunning attempts to dominate and use other people, the play is remarkably funny, although the audience is often seduced into laughing at something that in immediate retrospect is far from funny.

According to Lenny, Max, like Disson in *Tea Party*, is obsessed by the need for order and clarity. Ash trays are regularly used, cleaned, and tidied away, and, at the beginning of Act Two, the coffee cups, small and elegant, are neatly returned to the tray as the family leaves. The place is as bare and clean as is the room after the dwarfs have left in the play bearing their name. Thus, Lenny, who resembles Mick in *The Caretaker*, also resembles Len and Aston. The difference is that Lenny is not anguished. Nobody is driven by any higher emotion than greed or lust or hate.

The symbols seem clearer and almost pleasantly decorative. The three pools connect but, again, almost gratuitously, while Venice is invoked but not used. The characters have allegorical status, but it is scarcely felt: a butcher, pimp, boxer, and whore versus a chauffeur and philosopher, with the latter scarcely articulate and too passive to live in the energetic world of the other characters. *The Homecoming* is, therefore, a characteristic Pinter play, but it is also very much a new kind of play. The central theme *may* be that of *The Lover* (a woman is both wife and whore), but the husband is too unimportantly treated for this to be an accurate description. It *may* be possession (although each has his own room) as in *The Caretaker,* but *The Homecoming* is unredeemed by either compassion or humanity. All the rich sentiments of family affection that flow like treacle through the play are contradicted, ironic, phony—or all three.

Attitudes to the *status quo* emerge, and on none does the play seem to pass unequivocal judgment. Life being the black and greedy affair it is, one can act like Sam, who pretends to believe in goodness and probably dies for it, or like Ted, who refuses to get lost in the mess and turns his back on it. Or one can get lost in it and not mind, like Max and Joey. Or one can join the mess and beat the family at its own game, like Ruth. Lenny remains the enigmatic center of the play, neither free nor lost; he is seeking, half in jest, to know what is the difference, what merits reverence, what is truth. Yet Lenny is a pimp. The real play may, in a sense, be said to begin after the curtain falls; he and Ruth are measuring each other up for the fight that must ensue from the arrangements that the play has proposed.

CHAPTER 7

Conclusion

A WRITER must often pray to be saved from his critics and, not least, from those who admire him. When Dukore sums up the plays of Harold Pinter by saying that they have an "unreal reality" or a "realistic unreality," he seems to be assuming the right to paradox that is properly the artist's. Styan is not inaccurate in the following summary, but he is tactless:

> The correspondence between the fabulous province of Franz Kafka's mind and the nightmares of Beckett and Pinter grow [sic] more striking. Modern man falls helplessly before the inscrutable power of *The Castle* or of Godot or Goldberg. Time stands still as he becomes obsessed with his own soul, as in *The Trial*, and feels the ridiculous paralysis of living in infinity and eternity, like Joseph K. or Maddy, Didi or Gogo. In the teeth of coincidence and the unknown, the laws of nature crumble and distort, while a hostile and obscene universe arbitrarily transmogrifies him into a louse like Gregor Samsa in *Metamorphosis*, or puppet like Lucky or Davies, or into the despicable or pathetic animal of Hamm or Stanley.[1]

It is not simply that "puppet" strikes us as not quite accurate as a description of Davies so much as the juxtaposition of Davies and Lucky and what that juxtaposition implies. The confusion of Kafka, Beckett, and Pinter in one apocalyptic literary endeavor is unfair to all three, and particularly to Pinter; for an alignment of *The Castle*, Godot, and Goldberg is a declension (even if it were an accurate reading of Goldberg), like a comparison between absinthe and beer. As plays, and as themes, the differences between Beckett's *Waiting for Godot* and Pinter's *The Birthday Party* are too remarkable, and compared to Kafka, Pinter looks thin. He also looks sturdy and English.

There seems little value in lumping them together suggestively when the suggestions are a hindrance. True, that quality of mystery, which Wilson Knight characterizes as "numinous," is present in Pinter; but it is present in a particularly English way. Wilson Knight's description of this quality is perspicacious:

Harold Pinter's people are generally at cross-purposes with each other and sometimes tangled in a world of disconcerting objectivity. Mental discontinuities balance objective absurdities to arouse suspense and a sense of threat, bordering on insanity, as when in *The Dumb Waiter* mysterious orders for elaborate meals come down the lift from what had once been a restaurant to the basement kitchen where the two ambiguous ruffians are at their simultaneously flaccid and ominous talk; wherein perhaps a lucid symbolism may be felt flowering from a superficial absurdity. Pinter's conversation is usually that of lower middle-class normality, and the disconcerting objects those of town life and human fabrication. In *The Caretaker* Mick reels off a speech about London districts and its various bus-routes and then one about the legal and financial conditions of letting his property, in such a way as to make one dizzy. Questions may be left unanswered: who is the negro in *The Room*, who comes up from the basement of the tenement house, striking terror? Much of this is in the manner of Eugene Ionesco. What is so strange is that we are nowadays given the experience of nightmare, almost of the supernatural, in terms not of devils or ghosts, but of ordinary, material objects and affairs; and of people at cross-purposes with each other and with the audience in a paradoxical and dangerous world.[2]

Knight suggests that where life is less sophisticated—in the plays of Behan or Delaney—characters know where they are and what they want, and they have no difficulties in communication. But town life and the complexities of middle-class existence seem to produce terror; and the details of that life, with their false promises of preciseness, are part of that terror. Pinter is not in the least interested in proving something, as is Shaw or Wesker or even, as Osborne wishes to do, in providing what he considers to be the essential evidence. Pinter sets out to evoke rather than depict, to involve his audience in what Boulton has called "an imaginative comprehension of the dramatic situation, the seeming triviality of which masks its deeper significance."[3]
Language—that common to men and of common man—is employed to make us constantly aware of the essential loneliness of the human condition. In discussing or including remedies,

Conclusion

Pinter rarely indulges in overt speculation (like Beatie in *Roots* or like the reporter in *Under Plain Cover*). He attempts to show the constant effort of human beings to impress, confuse, or simply refuse to give answers about the problems that beset them, a refusal Pinter demonstrates in his plays.

Criticism of Pinter's work mainly stops short at *The Caretaker*, which remains, so far, the play in which Pinter has most successfully balanced life and mystery. Taylor describes the dialogue as "orchestrated naturalism"; for, beneath the faithful reproduction of the banality of average conversation, we catch unexpected resonances that give the talk weight and depth. Where Simpson merely exploits cliché, Pinter's usage of it fascinates and evolves; and this usage makes him of all contemporary British dramatists the most poetical—more so than either Fry or Eliot. Pinter has looked at the whole, not merely at the language, to find what Taylor calls "the strange sublunary poetry in ordinary things under a microscope":

At this stage all questions of realism or fantasy, naturalism or artifice become irrelevant, and indeed completely meaningless: whatever we think of his plays, whether we accept or reject them, they are monumentally and inescapably there, the artifact triumphantly separated from the artist, self-contained and self-supporting. Because he has achieved this, and he alone among British dramatists of our day, the conclusion seems inescapable that even if others may be more likeable, more approachable, more sympathetic to one's own personal tastes and convictions, in the long run he is likely to turn out the greatest of them all.[4]

Certainly, of all contemporary British dramatists only Pinter manages to be topical, local, and universal—to combine the European Absurd with native wit to create a record of common inevitability. Pinter says, modestly, of his own work: "I am very concerned with the shape and consistency of mood of my plays. I cannot write anything that appears to me to be loose and unfinished. I like a feeling of order in what I write."[5] This sense of order is the key to his work in any medium, and his success rests on it. In a very precise sense, among his contemporaries Pinter is the *miglior fabbro*.

Notes and References

Notes and References

Preface

1. Time has altered the situation. John Osborne's play *Inadmissable Evidence* opened at the Royal Court Theatre on September 9, 1964, followed by *A Patriot for Me* at the same theater which turned itself into a private club to avoid prosecution by the Lord Chamberlain; and in 1966 the National Theatre Company performed his latest play, *A Bond Honored*, a version of Lope de Vega's *La Fianza Satisfecha*. Harold Pinter has produced two new plays, but Brendan Behan died in 1964.

2. See also Sean O'Casey's rather sour dismissal in "The Bald Primaqueera" *Atlantic Monthly* (September, 1965). O'Casey does not appear to be very familiar with contemporary drama.

Chapter One

1. I am grateful to my colleague, A. M. Goldman, for drawing my attention to this play. *Hughie* (published, 1959) is more a play to be read than acted, since most of the meaning emerges from the stage directions. It was left to dramatists like Beckett and Pinter to translate the unspoken into dialogue.

2. J. L. Styan, *The Dark Comedy* (Cambridge, 1962), p. 192.

3. I am greatly indebted to Mr. William's article that was first published in *Twentieth Century*, CLXX, 1011, and revised for *The Pelican Guide to English Literature, The Modern Age*, No. 7 (London, 1961), pp. 496–508, under the title, "Recent English Drama."

4. The verse drama of Christopher Fry never presented such a challenge; its weakness was a strong tendency to use verse merely to decorate a romantic action rather than to create a new dramatic form. Fry has been more successful in producing verse drama than his avowed master T. S. Eliot, but only because Fry has avoided certain problems, the most crucial of which was to introduce to the majority theater serious considerations of serious problems and not simply making the audience laugh at a romantic situation deliberately kept unreal. *Curtmantle* (1961), Fry's most recent play, is, in fact, a play of ideas, argument, and seriousness, and the verse in it can be very flat indeed. Eliot's lucid style and sensibility drained his characters of vitality, and Fry has been no more successful. He did, however,

create an audience not unfavorable to poetic drama. Something more than what his plays offered was needed; the fantastic existence ornamented with verse yielded no poetic vision of life.

5. Dennis Welland, "Some Post-War Experiments in Poetic Drama," in William A. Armstrong (ed.), *Experimental Drama* (London, 1963), pp. 36ff. Dr. Welland, however, succumbs to the idea of noncommunication; Eliot should have taught him that humankind cannot bear very much reality; cf. Ionesco's reply to Esslin's question on this matter, *Observer* (September 1, 1963): "Communication is not only possible; it is easy; sometimes even too easy. No, what I am concerned about is that people are too lazy, too indolent to make the *effort* to communicate; that the tools of communication, language, have been allowed to fossilise into clichés and have lost the power to serve as instruments for genuine communication."

6. John Russell Taylor, *Anger and After* (London, 1963), pp. 115, 41.

7. John Mander, *The Writer and Commitment* (London, 1961), pp. 22, 180–81.

8. George E. Wellwarth, *The Theater of Protest and Paradox* (New York, 1964), pp. 225, 243.

9. Bamber Gascoigne, *Twentieth Century Drama* (London, 1962), p. 49.

10. Cf. Kenneth Tynan, *Tynan on Theater* (London, 1964). Tynan prefers Brecht and is not remarkably sympathetic to Absurd Theater, irked as he is by "their pervasive tone of privileged despair."

11. Walter Kaufmann, *Existentialism* (New York, 1956), p. 12. This anthology of Existentialist writing is very useful. But as the reader will no doubt gather, I do not find a philosophical ground in Pinter's work—except as all literature is grounded in thought.

12. "Dans les Armes de la Ville," *Cahiers de la Compagnie Madeleine Renaud Jean-Louis Barrault*, Paris, No. 20 (October, 1957), quoted Martin Esslin, *The Theater of the Absurd* (New York, 1961), p. xix.

13. Quoted in David Tutaev, "The Theater of the Absurd—How Absurd?" *Gambit*, No. 2 (n.d.), p. 70.

14. Lloyd Alexander (trans.), Jean-Paul Sartre's *Nausea* (London, 1962), p. 130.

15. *Ibid.*, pp. 171–72.

16. *Ibid.*, p. 173.

17. Iris Murdoch, *Sartre* (London, 1961), p. 13.

18. Esslin, *The Theater of the Absurd*, pp. 290–91.

19. R. D. Smith, "Back to the Text," in John R. Brown and Bernard Harris (eds.), *Contemporary Theater*, Stratford-on-Avon Studies, No. 4 (London, 1965), p. 135.

20. "Harold Pinter Replies," *New Theatre Magazine*, XI, 2 (January, 1961), pp. 8–10.

21. F. N. Lees, "Samuel Beckett," *Manchester Memoirs*, CIV, 4 (1961–1962).

22. Tynan, *Tynan on Theater*, p. 63.

23. See Robert Brustein, *The Theater of Revolt* (London, 1965), Chap. VII.

24. See D. Krause, *Sean O'Casey, The Man and His Work* (London, 1960), Chap. 2, where the bastard genre is discussed as one of the forms of twentieth-century drama. Dramatists as varied as Shakespeare, Chekhov, Shaw, Synge, O'Casey, Pirandello, Giradoux, Anouilh, Sartre, Wilder, Beckett, and Ionesco are all shown to have used music hall devices!

25. "Harold Pinter Replies," cf. *New Comment* (October, 1963), British Broadcasting Corporation, "Third Program." Pinter discussed his relationship with Beckett, describing his first contact with him, reading the novel *Watt*, as an absolute knockout; the plays of Beckett came later.

26. Martin Esslin, "Godot and His Children," in Armstrong, *Experimental Drama*, pp. 128ff. The quotations appear on pp. 136–37 and 140. The essay is very much in the same direction as the essay on Pinter in *The Theater of the Absurd*.

27. Styan, *The Dark Comedy*, pp. 234–35.

28. *Ibid.*, pp. 235–36.

29. Wellwarth, *The Theater of Protest and Paradox*, pp. 212–20, thinks more highly of Simpson than I do. He suggests in his last sentence that of all current dramatists, Simpson is closest in spirit to Jarry himself.

30. Tutaev, "The Theater of the Absurd—How Absurd?", pp. 68–70.

31. Robert Bolt, interviewed in *Plays and Players* (December, 1963), p. 11.

32. "Writing for Myself," *Twentieth Century*, CLXIX, 1008 (February, 1961), pp. 172–75. This article, ironically, was not written by Pinter but compiled by Findlater from the tape of an interview. Mr. Pinter has always regarded this article as unsatisfactory.

Chapter Two

1. "Writing for Myself." See Note 32, Chapter I.

2. *The Observer* profile (September 15, 1963) attributed the name "da Pinta" to Pinter's Portuguese ancestry. But Pinter himself, in a letter to me dated April 28, 1964, pointed out that this was very remote.

3. David Campton, quoted Taylor, *Anger and After*, p. 165.

4. J. T. Boulton, "Harold Pinter; *The Caretaker* and Other Plays," *Modern Drama* (September, 1963), pp. 131–140, produces this excellent conception.

5. Interview by Hallam Tennyson, British Broadcasting Corporation General Overseas Service, August 7, 1960, quoted in Esslin, *The Theater of the Absurd*, p. 199.

6. Interview by Tynan, British Broadcasting Corporation Home Service, October 28, 1960, quoted in Esslin, *The Theater of the Absurd*, p. 199.

7. Esslin, *The Theater of the Absurd*, p. 201.

8. *Ibid.*, p. 200.

9. Clifford Leech, "Two Romantics: Arnold Wesker and Harold Pinter," in Brown and Harris, *Contemporary Theater*, p. 26.

10. "Harold Pinter Replies."

11. John Bowen, "Accepting the Illusion," *Twentieth Century*, CLXIX, 1008 (February, 1961), p. 162.

12. *The Room* (New York, 1961), p. 99.

13. *Ibid.*, p. 110.

14. *Ibid.*, p. 118.

15. Wellwarth, *The Theater of Protest and Paradox*, p. 200.

16. Taylor, *Anger and After*, p. 287.

17. Ruby Cohn, "The World of Harold Pinter," *Tulane Drama Review*, VI, 3 (March, 1962), pp. 55–68.

18. Boulton, "Harold Pinter: *The Caretaker* and Other Plays," pp. 131–40.

19. Irving Wardle, *Encore* (July-August, 1958), pp. 39–40.

20. Jacqueline Hoefer, "Pinter and Whiting: Two Attitudes Towards The Alienated Artist," *Modern Drama*, IV (1962), pp. 402–8.

21. *The Birthday Party* (New York, 1961), p. 32.

22. Cf. the gloss of this device in Jack Kerouac, *The Town and the City* (New York, 1950), pp. 375ff.

23. *The Birthday Party*, p. 54.

24. *Ibid.*, p. 59.

25. *Ibid.*, p. 80.

26. *Ibid.*, pp. 82–3.

27. *Ibid.*, p. 84.

28. *Ibid.*, p. 88.

29. Clifford Leech, "Two Romantics: Arnold Wesker and Harold Pinter," in Brown and Harris, *Contemporary Theater*, pp. 11–31.

30. Gregorz Sinko, "Stara i Młoda Anglia," *Dialog*, LX, 4 (April, 1961), pp. 97–99.

31. Esslin, *The Theater of the Absurd*, p. 203.

32. *Ibid.*, p. 205.

33. Gascoigne, *Twentieth Century Drama*, p. 206.
34. Wellwarth, *The Theater of Protest and Paradox*, p. 201ff.
35. Tynan interview, Esslin, *The Theater of the Absurd*, p. 205; Tennyson interview, ibid., p. 205.
36. Tynan interview, Esslin, *The Theater of the Absurd*, p. 207.
37. Styan, *The Dark Comedy*, p. 236.
38. Bernard Dukore, "The Theater of Harold Pinter," *Tulane Drama Review*, VI, 3 (March, 1962), pp. 55–68.
39. Wilson Knight, "The Kitchen Sink," *Encounter*, XXI, 6 (December, 1963), pp. 48–54.
40. James T. Boulton, "Harold Pinter: The Caretaker and Other Plays," *Modern Drama* (September, 1963), pp. 131–140.
41. Taylor, *Anger and After*, p. 290.
42. *Ibid.*, p. 291.
43. Sinko, "Stara i Młoda Anglia," pp. 97–99.
44. *The Dumb Waiter* (New York, 1961), pp. 102–3.
45. Tom Maschler (ed.) *New English Dramatists*, No. 3, Introduction by J. W. Lambert, pp. 9–10.
46. *A Slight Ache* (New York, 1962), p. 35.
47. John Russell Brown, "Mr. Pinter's Shakespeare," *Critical Quarterly*, V, 3 (Autumn, 1963), pp. 251–65.
48. See Chapter Five for discussion of "Tea Party."
49. "The Examination," in *The Collection and The Lover* (London, 1963), pp. 89–94.
50. *A Slight Ache and Other Plays* (London, 1961), p. 121.
51. Recorded by Kenneth Williams. See bibliography.
52. Quoted in Taylor, *Anger and After*, p. 296.
53. Laurence Kitchin, "Backwards and Forwards," *Twentieth Century*, CLXIX, 1008, p. 168.
54. *A Slight Ache and Other Plays*, p. 47.
55. *Ibid.*, p. 87.
56. Taylor, *Anger and After*, p. 307.
57. Wellwarth, *The Theater of Protest and Paradox*, p. 208.
58. "Writing for Myself."
59. *Ibid.*
60. Cf. the following extract from Sartre's *Nausea, op. cit.*, p. 169.

I murmur: "It's a seat," a little like an exorcism. But the word stays on my lips: it refuses to go and put itself on the things. It stays what it is, with its red plush, thousands of little red paws in the air, all still, little dead paws, this belly floating in this car, in this grey sky, is not a seat. It could just as well be a dead donkey tossed about in the water, floating with the current, belly in the air in a great grey river, a river of floods; and I could be sitting on the donkey's belly, my feet dangling in the clear water. Things are divorced from their names. They are there, grotesque, headstrong, gigantic and it seems ridiculous to call them seats or say anything at all about them: I am in the midst of things, nameless things. Alone, without words, defenceless, they surround me, are beneath me, behind me, above me. They demand nothing, they don't impose themselves: they are there.

61. Wellwarth, *The Theater of Protest and Paradox*, p. 208.

62. Phrases like "butter's up" and "gentleman's gentleman" recur in *The Servant*. It is surely the poet in Pinter that leads to these recurrences of phrase and image.

63. *The Dwarfs* (New York, 1962), p. 91.

64. *Ibid.*, pp. 99–100, 101.

65. *Ibid.*, pp. 103–4.

66. *Ibid.*, p. 108.

67. B.B.C. Transcript, *New Comment* (this accounts for the oddness of punctuation and the erratic grammar of the passages quoted).

68. Murdoch, *Sartre*, p. 35.

69. Taylor, *Anger and After*, pp. 307–8.

70. Tynan interview, Esslin, *The Theater of the Absurd*, p. 216.

71. Esslin, *The Theater of the Absurd*, p. 215.

72. Tynan interview, *ibid.*, p. 216.

Chapter Three

1. Leech, "Two Romantics: Arnold Wesker and Harold Pinter," p. 14.

2. Kitchin, "Backwards and Forwards," *Twentieth Century*, CLXIX, 1008, pp. 168–9.

3. "Writing for Myself."

4. Laurence Kitchin, *Mid-Century Drama* (London, 1960), p. 114.

5. Esslin, *The Theater of the Absurd*, p. 213.

6. "Harold Pinter Replies."

7. Tynan interview, Esslin, *The Theater of the Absurd*, p. 212.

8. "Jig saw" also means pieces to be fitted together into a picture.

9. *The Caretaker* (New York, 1961), p. 34.

10. *Ibid.*, p. 46.

11. *Ibid.*, p. 60.

12. *Ibid.*, pp. 63–64.

13. *Ibid.*, p. 70.

14. *Ibid.*, p. 76.

15. *Ibid.*, p. 77.

Notes and References

16. The film more or less followed the Samuel French Acting Edition at this point, inserting dialogue:

MICK *and* ASTON *look at each other then both smile faintly.*
MICK *tentatively indicates the pieces of the broken Buddha.*
MICK: Look I . . .
(ASTON *regards the pieces then looks at* MICK.) Look, what about
. . . .
(MICK *breaks off, goes to door and exits, leaving it open.*) The great difficulty, not present in the film anyway, is for the smile between the two brothers to be seen. Some dialogue might help in the theater.

17. I am grateful for conversations with Sister Margaret Parkes and Dr. T. Grant, of the Student Health Center, University of Manchester, on the subject of shock treatment then and now. I am assured that under the circumstances there is no reason to feel that Pinter is being medically inaccurate.
18. It is surely no accident that Donner took Bates into his next film, *Nothing But the Best*, the story of the rise to fame and wealth of a smooth-tongued Cockney boy who is also sinister in his ambitions and methods.
19. "Filming 'The Caretaker'," *Transatlantic Review*, No. 13 (Summer, 1963), pp. 17–26.
20. B.B.C. Transcript, *New Comment* (see note 67, Chapter 2).
21. John Russell Taylor, *Sight and Sound* (Winter, 1963), pp. 38–39.
22. Taylor, *Anger and After*, pp. 299–302.
23. *Ibid.*, p. 300.
24. *Ibid.*, p. 301.
25. John Arden, *New Theater Magazine*, I, 4 (July, 1960), pp. 29–30.
26. Ruby Cohn, "The World of Harold Pinter," pp. 55–68.
27. Kay Dick, "Mr. Pinter and the Fearful Matter," *Texas Quarterly*, IV, 3 (Autumn, 1961), pp. 257–65.
28. Wilson Knight, "The Kitchen Sink," *Encounter*, XXI, 6 (December, 1963), pp. 48–54.
29. Leech, "Two Romantics: Arnold Wesker and Harold Pinter," p. 29.
30. Gascoigne, *Twentieth Century Drama*, p. 54.
31. Boulton, "Harold Pinter: The Caretaker and Other Plays," pp. 131–40.
32. The word "tramp" should not be used too significantly. Davies is simply called in the text "an old man." Although he claims to have

been "on the road a few years," he is now very much a denizen of the city and is static. As such, it seems dangerous to put too much stress on him as "free" in the sense that a tramp may be said to be. He works, after all, in cafés. Cf. Dick, "Mr. Pinter and the Fearful Matter," where she points out that Davies is not so much one of Beckett's dispossessed beggars as a person without social security.

33. Wellwarth, *The Theater of Protest and Paradox*, p. 207.

34. Sinko, "Stara i Młoda Anglia," pp. 97–99.

Chapter Four

1. Taylor, *Anger and After*, p. 198.

2. Leech, "Two Romantics: Arnold Wesker and Harold Pinter," pp. 16–17.

3. "Writing for Myself."

4. *Ibid.*

5. John Bowen, "Accepting the Illusion," *Twentieth Century*, CLXIX, 1008 (February, 1961), p. 162.

6. "Harold Pinter Replies."

7. James's surname is "Horne," which has implications of cuckoldry.

8. *The Collection* (New York, 1962), pp. 77–78.

9. This, like the crucial smile in *The Caretaker*, is a difficult action to capture outside television; in the Stoke-on-Trent production (in the round), at least half the audience is necessarily seeing her back. It is doubtful whether or not any conventional stage could get over this final enigmatic close-up.

10. John Russell Taylor, *Plays and Players* (August, 1962), p. 20.

11. Taylor, *Anger and After* (London, 1962), p. 255.

12. Taylor, *Anger and After* (London, 1963), p. 311.

13. Alex M. Cain, *The Tablet* (June 30, 1962), pp. 624–25.

14. *The Lover* (London, 1963), p. 57.

15. *Ibid.*, p. 71.

16. *Ibid.*, p. 74.

17. *Ibid.*, p. 83.

18. Anthony Storr, *Sexual Deviations* (Harmondsworth, 1964), p. 40.

19. The stage direction in the text reads: *She strokes his neck and the back of his head.* In Pinter's production, she stroked and fondled his knee and thigh.

20. Taylor, *Anger and After*, pp. 311–12.

21. *Ibid.*

22. An amateur production in Manchester interpreted the play differently. The program note read:

> In an attempt to make his wife admit the true nature of their relationship, the husband becomes a menacing figure: he torments his wife, reduces her to a state of complete confusion and only then discovers how utterly dependent she has become upon the unreality they have created together. His attempt fails, and they sink into a different kind of unreality.

This interpretation runs counter to Pinter's production, and, if feasible, strikes me as less satisfying.

Chapter Five

1. *Isis*, 1456 (February 1, 1964) devoted the whole issue to the film *The Servant*, printing a deleted scene in which Barrett returns to his digs after being hired (he has been sleeping with his landlady). Two articles discuss Losey's work, showing that the film's themes are his as well as Pinter's. The tone of some of these articles leads one to suspect a little leg-pulling on the part of those interviewed!
2. B.B.C. *New Comment* (see Note 67, Chapter 2).
3. Robin Maugham, *The Servant* (London, 1964), p. 21.
4. *Ibid.*, p. 22.
5. "Joseph Losey and 'The Servant,' " *Film*, 38, p. 29.
6. *The Servant*, Release Script, 4/3.
7. *Ibid.*, 3/1.
8. Maugham, *The Servant*, p. 25.
9. *The Servant*, Release Script, 9/5.
10. "Joseph Losey and 'The Servant,' " p. 28.
11. Maugham, *The Servant*, pp. 12, 45.
12. *The Servant*, Release Script, 4/4.
13. *Ibid.*, 4/9.
14. *Ibid.*, 4/6.
15. *Ibid.*, 5/3.
16. John Russell Taylor, *Sight and Sound* (Winter, 1963/4), pp. 38–39.
17. Evergreen Productions could not raise the money to shoot the three scripts, so they shot one, Beckett's scenario. This, called simply *Film*, is directed by Alan Schneider and performed (with his back to the camera for all except the last shot, apparently) by Buster Keaton. See *Tulane Drama Review*, Vol. 9, No. 3 (Spring, 1965), pp. 118ff.
18. The text reads "Sisson," which Pinter prefers. But it appears that there is a manufacturer of sanitary ware in Sheffield called Sisson.

Chapter Six

1. *The Homecoming* (London, 1965), p. 62.
2. *Ibid.*, p. 20.
3. *Ibid.*, p. 40.
4. *Ibid.*, p. 9.
5. *Ibid.*, p. 9.
6. *Ibid.*, p. 37.
7. *Ibid.*, p. 42.
8. *Ibid.*, p. 46.
9. This speech was altered in production. The original script read:

Because we know something about the values which have been handed down to us. We may be a little dull, but we still have an eye for mother nature, and often in fact sit out in the back yard having a quiet gander at the night sky. Our little community, our quiet little group, our team, you might say, our unit, made up of, I'll admit it, various and not entirely similar component parts, but which, put together, do nevertheless make up a whole. An organism, which, though we're not exactly a sentimental family, we do recognize as such. And you're an integral part of it, Ted. When we all sit out there in the backyard looking up at the night sky, often as not there's an empty chair standing in the circle, which is in fact yours. And so when you at length return to us, we do expect a bit of grace, a bit of je ne sais quoi, a bit of generosity of mind, a bit of liberality of spirit, to reassure us. We do expect that. But do we get it? Have we got it? Is that what you've given us?

10. *The Homecoming*, p. 29.
11. *Ibid.*, p. 52.
12. *Ibid.*, pp. 61–62.

Chapter Seven

1. Styan, *The Dark Comedy*, p. 238.
2. Knight, "The Kitchen Sink," pp. 48–54.
3. Boulton, "Harold Pinter: *The Caretaker* and Other Plays," pp. 131–40.
4. Taylor, *Anger and After*, p. 315.
5. "Harold Pinter Replies."

Selected Bibliography

Selected Bibliography

PRIMARY SOURCES

Harold Pinter is published by Grove Press in America and by Methuen in England. There is also available in England "Acting Editions" published by Samuel French where certain textual differences occur because of the nature of these editions (they are for amateur productions). In one instance only in this work is this third edition important, and in that instance the note specifies that the French edition has been quoted. Elsewhere, for the convenience of readers, the Grove Press editions have been used, where available, and pagination in the notes shows this. In the case of other plays, not as yet published in America, the Methuen editions have been used.

The Birthday Party and The Room. New York: Grove Press, Inc., 1961.

The Caretaker and *The Dumb Waiter.* New York: Grove Press, Inc., 1961.

Three Plays: A Slight Ache, The Collection, The Dwarfs. New York: Grove Press, Inc., 1962.

The Birthday Party and Other Plays. London: Methuen & Co., Ltd., 1960. Includes *The Birthday Party, The Room* and *The Dumb Waiter.*

The Caretaker. London: Methuen & Co., Ltd., 1960. A recording of the sound track of the film of *The Caretaker* is available on Oriole, M.G. 20093–4.

A Slight Ache and Other Plays. London: Methuen & Co., Ltd., 1961. Includes *A Slight Ache, A Night Out, The Dwarfs* and the following revue sketches: "Trouble in the Works," "The Black and White," "Request Stop," "Last to Go," and "Applicant." A recording of "Last to Go" by Kenneth Williams is available on "Pieces of Eight," Decca SKL 4084, and "Kenneth Williams," Decca DFE 8548.

The Collection and The Lover. London: Methuen & Co., Ltd., 1963. Also includes the short prose piece "The Examination," first published in *Prospect* (Summer, 1959), pp. 21–25.

The Homecoming. London: Methuen & Co., Ltd., 1965.

Tea Party and Other Plays. London: Methuen & Co., Ltd., 1967. Includes *Tea Party, The Basement,* and *Night School.*

The following poems were published in *Poetry London*: "New Year in the Midlands," "Chandeliers and Shadows," 19 (August, 1950); "New Year in the Midlands," "Rural Idyll," "European Revels," 20 (November, 1950), and "One a Story, Two a Death," in 22 (Summer, 1951). A footnote reads that a typographical error in No. 19 caused the reprinting of "New Year in the Midlands" in No. 20. In both No. 20 and No. 22 Harold Pinter is printed as Harold Pinta.

The following prose articles and stories are available:

"Harold Pinter Replies," *New Theater Magazine*, XI, 2 (January, 1961), pp. 8–10.

"Writing for Myself," *Twentieth Century*, CLXIX, 1008, (London: February, 1961), pp. 172–75. This issue also contains a poem by Pinter.

"Harold Pinter and Clive Donner on filming *The Caretaker*." *Transatlantic Review*, 13 (London: Summer, 1963), pp. 17–23.

"Dialogue for Three," *Stand* (Leeds: 1963–1964).

"Writing for the Theater," *Evergreen Review*, 33 (August-September, 1964), pp. 80–82.

"Tea Party," broadcast British Broadcasting Corporation, "Third Program," (1964), published in *Playboy* (January, 1965).

"The Black and White," *Flourish* (Summer, 1965). *Flourish* is the magazine of the Royal Shakespeare Theater Club, and this piece (dated 1955) is a prose version of the sketch of the same name. "The Black and White" is reprinted in *Transatlantic Review*, 21 (Summer, 1966), pp. 51–52.

"The Art of the Theater III," *The Paris Review*, No. 39, pp. 13-37. Interview of Harold Pinter by Lawrence M. Bensky.

Unpublished Work

Apart from the film scripts of *The Servant, The Pumpkin Eater, The Quiller Memorandum* and *Accident*, the following items have not been published: "Special Offer," and "Getting Acquainted"—two revue sketches from *Pieces of Eight* (1959); "That's All," "Interview," and "That's Your Trouble," these three revue sketches broadcast in April and May, 1964, by the British Broadcasting Corporation, "Third Program."

SECONDARY SOURCES

I. *General Works*

Armstrong, William A. (ed.) *Experimental Drama*. London: G. Bell and Sons Ltd., 1963. Extension lectures given at the University of London rewritten in essay form; the essay on Pinter by Esslin reflects the section in *The Theater of the Absurd*.

Selected Bibliography

Bentley, Eric. *The Playwright as Thinker*. Cleveland: World Publishing Co., 1955. This "study of the modern theater" stops short of Pinter, but it is an excellent survey of the predecessors of our theater, showing the existence of Absurd and Cruel Theater before the present day.

Brown, John R. and Harris, Bernard (eds.) *Contemporary Theater*. Stratford-on-Avon Studies, No. 4. London: Edward Arnold Ltd., 1962. Nine essays on various aspects of contemporary theater. Leech's essay on Wesker and Pinter is useful.

Brustein, Robert. *The Theater of Revolt*. London: Methuen & Co., Ltd., 1965. Rebellion in the theater in the work of eight outstanding playwrights from Ibsen to Genet. The chapter on Pirandello is particularly useful in a study of Pinter.

Chiari, Joseph. *Landmarks of Contemporary Drama*. London: Herbert Jenkins, 1965. A survey of the last forty years of drama useful for its critical examination of labels like "Theater of the Absurd."

Esslin, Martin. *The Theater of the Absurd*. New York: Doubleday & Co., 1961. The seminal work on this genre of theater, its philosophy and drama.

Esslin, Martin. *Absurd Drama*. London: Penguin Books, Ltd., 1965. Esslin's introduction to the four plays in this volume is, in brief space, a sensible explanation of Absurd Theater. Less extravagant in its scope and claims, it is perhaps more persuasive than the earlier book.

Gascoigne, Bamber. *Twentieth Century Drama*. London: Hutchinson & Co., Ltd., 1962. A readable survey of drama, particularly interesting on the Surrealist Drama of the 1920's.

Grossvogel, David I. *Four Playwrights and a Postscript*. Ithaca: Cornell University Press, 1962. This study of the plays of Brecht, Ionesco, Beckett, and Genet as "blasphemers" is interesting because it brings Brechtian theater into a relationship with Theater of the Absurd.

Hall, Adam. *The Quiller Memorandum*. London: Collins & Co., Ltd., 1965. The book of the film.

Kaufmann, Walter. ed. *Existentialism from Dostoevsky to Sartre*. New York: World Publishing Co., Meridian Books, 1956. An anthology of the basic writings of existentialism, the philosophy which is, apparently, behind Absurd Drama.

Kitchin, Laurence. *Mid-Century Drama*. London: Faber and Faber, Ltd., 1960. A readable literary history that serves as a useful, if pedestrian, introduction to the period.

Mander, John. *The Writer and Commitment*. London: Secker and Warburg, Ltd., 1961. Mander examines the very complex problem of "commitment" in literature. This is useful because commitment is the source of Brecht and Angry Theater, while the Absurd Theater remains uncommitted. This study shows that the problem of definition is not simple.

Maugham, Robin. *The Servant.* London: William Heinemann, Ltd., 1964. The novel from which Pinter adapted the script for the film of the same name.

Mortimer, Penelope. *The Pumpkin Eater.* London: Hutchinson & Co., Ltd., 1962. The book of the film.

Mosley, Nicholas. *Accident.* London: Hodder & Stoughton Ltd., 1965. The book of the film.

Murdoch, Iris. *Sartre.* London: Bowes and Bowes, Ltd., 1961. A perceptive study of Sartre's work, particularly good on *Nausea.*

Sartre, Jean-Paul. *Nausea.* London: Hamish Hamilton, 1962. Translated by Lloyd Alexander, this novel captures the existentialist attitude to life and demonstrates what Esslin has called "Absurdity."

Styan, J. L. *The Dark Comedy.* Cambridge: Cambridge University Press, 1962. As the title implies, this book traces the history, and particularly the modern development, of the comic tragedy.

Taylor, John R. *Anger and After.* London: Methuen & Co., Ltd., 1962; revised, Penguin Books, Ltd., 1963. The indispensable survey of contemporary British theater, the only study that is perceptive, comprehensive, and well written.

Trewin, J. C. *Drama in Britain.* London: Longman, Green and Co., 1965. A British Council Pamphlet with a checklist of plays since 1951, a useful survey in limited space.

Tynan, Kenneth. *Tynan on Theater.* London: Penguin Books, Ltd., 1964. Selection of reviews anthologized by Tynan himself. Interesting because Tynan dislikes Absurd Theater and says so.

Wellwarth, George E. *The Theater of Protest and Paradox.* New York: New York University Press, 1964. A discussion of developments in recent drama that includes both Angry and Absurd playwrights. Excellent bibliographies for individual playwrights.

II. *Magazines*

Marovitz, Charles, Milne, Tom, and Hale, Owen (eds.) *The Encore Reader.* London: Methuen & Co., Ltd., 1965. This reprints reviews and articles from the magazine *Encore.* Crucial reviews of Pinter are on p. 76 and p. 129. *Encore* disappeared at the end of 1965; it has now, apparently, been incorporated, together with *Theater World,* into *Play and Players.* A new magazine, *Jury,* appeared on December 6, 1965, reprinting reviews of important productions without editorial comment. After only eight issues this magazine has ceased to appear. *Tulane Drama Review,* XI, 2 (Winter, 1966) is devoted to "British Theatre, 1956-66," contains two articles on Pinter and is generally useful on the period with which we are concerned.

III. *Articles*

Bernhard, F. J. "Beyond Realism: The Plays of Harold Pinter." *Modern Drama,* III, 2 (September, 1965), pp. 185-91. Discusses symbols and rhythms in dialogue that although apparently realistic and dealing with realistic situations, becomes something more than realism.

Boulton, James T. "Harold Pinter: *The Caretaker* and Other Plays," *Modern Drama* VI, 2 (September, 1963), pp. 131-40. The best single article on Pinter's plays, up to and including *The Caretaker,* covering themes and method.

Brown, John Russell. "Mr. Pinter's Shakespeare," *Critical Quarterly,* V, 3 (Autumn, 1963), pp. 251-65. Uses Pinter's method—the absence of exposition, development, and conclusion in the formal sense—to look at Shakespeare again. Illuminates both Pinter and Shakespeare (with a look at Beckett and Ionesco en route).

Brown, John Russell. "Dialogue in Pinter and Others," *Critical Quarterly,* VII, 3 (Autumn, 1965), pp. 225-43. Taking the point of view suggested in the article above, Brown examines the dialogue in Pinter's plays as an example of Stanislavsky's "sub-text."

Cohn, Ruby. "The World of Harold Pinter," *Tulane Drama Review,* VI, 3 (March, 1962), pp. 55-68. Shows the first four plays as a developing allegory about annihilation: victim versus society. Her choice of victim seems curious, particularly in her analysis of *The Caretaker.*

Dick, Kay. "Mr. Pinter and the Fearful Matter," *Texas Quarterly,* IV, 3 (Autumn, 1961), pp. 257-65. A reading of the plays as a sequence in which violence is gradually eliminated and passive resistance triumphs in *The Caretaker.* Such analysis overlooks the crucial suffering of Aston in that play. Dick makes, however, an important distinction between Davies and the tramps of Samuel Beckett.

Dukore, Bernard. "The Theater of Harold Pinter," *Tulane Drama Review,* VI, 3 (March, 1962), pp. 43-54. Pinter's plays reflect the tensions and attitudes of present-day England, which is no longer a colonial power, and show man as an individual being reduced to a cipher.

Hoefer, Jacqueline. "Pinter and Whiting: Two Attitudes Towards the Alienated Artist," *Modern Drama,* IV (February, 1962), pp.

402–8. A very interesting comparison between two plays about a birthday (*Saint's Day* and *The Birthday Party*), both of which treat the artist alienated from society.

Knight, Wilson. "The Kitchen Sink," *Encounter*, XXI, 6 (December, 1963), pp. 48–54. Examines the contrast between a dynamic outsider and civilized man in contemporary drama. His interpretation of *The Caretaker* is not supported by the text.

Morris, Kelly. "The Homecoming." *Tulane Drama Review*, XI, 2 (Winter, 1966), pp. 185-91. An analysis of *The Homecoming* as a type of modern comedy of manners showing aggressive dialogue within a format of excessive decorum; the theme is the restoration, through Ruth, of a matriarchy.

Schechner, Richard. "Puzzling Pinter." *Tulane Drama Review*, XI, 2 (Winter, 1966), pp. 176-84. Discusses the "incompleteness" of Pinter's plays, suggesting that, as a disinterested artist, Pinter is asking: what can the theater do? The realistic attention of the audience focused on an illusionistic presentation leads to an insoluble riddle.

Sinko, Gregorz. "Stara i Młoda Anglia," *Dialogue*, LX, 4 (April, 1961), pp. 97–99. Discusses three early plays of Pinter as in the tradition of Franz Kafka. Not, unfortunately, translated from the Polish.

Tutaev, David. "The Theater of the Absurd . . . How Absurd?" *Gambit*, No. 2 (n.d.), pp. 68–70. Asks where Absurd Theater is going and suggests it is a facet of Romanticism incompatible with our times.

Williams, Raymond. "Recent English Drama," *The Pelican Guide to English Literature*, No. 7, *The Modern Age* (London, 1961), pp. 496–508. Excellent survey of the dramatic situation in England, with a short bibliography.

Index

Index

Absurd Theater, 21, 26-37, 40, 88, 165

Adamov, Arthur, 23; *L'Invasion*, 34

Addams, Charles, 57

Albee, Edward, 21, 27; *The Zoo Story*; 33, *Who's Afraid of Virginia Woolf?*, 33, 124

Andreyev, Leonid, 32

Angry Theater, 21, 24-26

Arden, John, 34, 35, 102; *Live Like Pigs*, 24

Artaud, Antonin, 26, 34, 56

Beckett, Samuel, 21, 23, 27, 30, 32, 33, 35, 42, 57, 109, 135, 163; *Waiting for Godot*, 26, 31, 33, 34, 36, 40-41, 60, 91, 105, 163; *End-Game*, 41; *Film*, 138

Behan, Brendan, 164

Bolt, Robert, 36

Brecht, Bertolt, 21, 23, 27, 36, 41; *Baal*, 32; *Mother Courage and Her Children*, 62

Campton, David, 34, 35; *The Lunatic View*, 40

Camus, Albert, *The Myth of Sisyphus*, 27

Chaplin, Charles, 34

Chekhov, Anton, 41, 88

Cocteau, Jean, *The Bridal Pair at the Eiffel Tower*, 32

Commitment, the problem of, 25, 30

Cruelty, Theater of, 26

cummings, e. e., *HIM*, 32

Dadaism, 32

Delaney, Shelagh, 164; *A Taste of Honey*, 24

Dostoevsky, Fyodor, 27

Eliot, T. S., 22-23, 46, 57, 165; *Sweeney Agonistes*, 22, 32

Euripides, 33

Existentialism, 27-32

Fry, Christopher, 165

Gelber, Jack, 27

Genet, Jean, 27, 30, 114

Golding, William, 35

Gorki, Maxim, 57, 88

Greene, Graham, 59, 109

Heidegger, Martin, 27

Hemingway, Ernest, 88

Ionesco, Eugène, 23, 27, 28, 30, 31, 35, 40, 88, 135, 164; *The Bald Prima Donna*, 31; *The Chairs*, 41; *The Killer*, 70

Jarry, Alfred, *Ubu Roi*, 26, 32

Jaspers, 27

Kafka, Franz, 27, 41, 54, 55, 59, 88, 163

Kierkegaard, 27

Laurel and Hardy, 34

Livings, Henry, *Nil Carborundum*, 62

Marlowe, Christopher, 33

Molière, 33

Murdoch, Iris, 35; *Sartre*, 29, 84, 85; *A Severed Head*, 117

Mystery Plays, 33

Nietzsche, 27

O'Neill, Eugene, 21

Orton, Joe, *Loot*, 158

Osborne, John, 23, 30, 35, 36, 124, 164; *Look Back in Anger*, 24, 25, 26; *The Entertainer*, 24; *Under Plain Cover*, 33, 123, 124, 165

Pascal, Blaise, 27

Pinter, Harold, 21, 23, 27, 32, 34, 163, 165; violence in adolescence,

40; commitment as a writer, 25, 30, 37; poetry, 38-40; compared with Simpson, 35, 42, 165; influenced by Beckett, 33-34, 135; writing for television, 108-10, 118-19

WRITINGS OF:

The Room, 38, 40, 41-48, 50, 52, 67, 68, 73, 88, 106, 137, 146, 147, 160, 164
The Birthday Party, 38, 40, 41, 48-63, 64, 68, 73, 74, 75, 81, 87, 106, 107, 108, 117, 118, 152, 163
The Dumb Waiter, 33, 38, 50, 51, 55, 63-68, 69, 73, 75, 79, 89, 164
A Slight Ache, 68-71, 73, 75, 84, 85, 89, 109, 125, 126, 144
"The Examination," 71-73
The Dwarfs, 28, 68, 70, 73, 75, 78-86, 87, 101, 117, 159
A Night Out, 75-78, 108, 110, 112, 114, 144
The Caretaker, 31, 37, 42, 61, 63, 70, 71, 74, 75, 78, 85, 86, 87-107, 108, 146, 153, 156, 160, 161, 162, 164, 165
Film of The Caretaker, 96-100, 126
The Collection, 71, 86, 110, 111, 114-18, 142, 160
The Lover, 33, 71, 83, 84, 109, 110, 111, 114, 117, 118-24, 134, 142, 160, 161
Tea Party (story), 125-26; (play), 138-45, 146, 148, 153, 157, 160
The Homecoming, 138, 144, 146-62
The Basement (originally The Compartment), 126, 135-38

SKETCHES:

"Special Offer," 73-74
"Getting Acquainted," 74
"Trouble in the Works," 74
"The Black and White," 74

"Last to Go," 75
"Request Stop," 75
"Dialogue for Three," 125
"That's All," 125
"That's Your Trouble," 125
"Interview," 125

FILMS:

The Servant, 71, 111, 126, 127-33, 137
The Pumpkin Eater, 126, 127, 133-35
The Quiller Memorandum, 126
Accident, 126

Pirandello, Luigi, 32; The Rules of the Game, 32-33
Poetic drama, 21, 22-24
Pound, Ezra, 22

Rilke, 27, 28

Sartre, Jean-Paul, 23, 27, 30; Nausea, 28-30, 84; Huis Clos, 41; The Respectful Prostitute, 48; Altona, 84
Saunders, James, 30
Shaffer, Peter, Five Finger Exercise, 148
Shakespeare, 33
Shaw, G. B., 164
Simpson, N. F., 30, 34, 40; compared with Pinter, 35, 42, 165
Storr, Anthony, Sexual Deviations, 122
Strindberg, August, 32
Surrealism, 32

Tardieu, Jean, Qui est là?, 34
Thomas, Dylan, 39

Wedekind, Frank, 32
Wesker, Arnold, 23, 30, 35, 164; Trilogy, 25, 62, 165; Chips with Everything, 62
Whiting, John, Saint's Day, 50
Williams, Tennessee, 27, 31

Yeats, W. B., 22